PLANNING YOUR
Organic
HERB GARDEN

By the same author

PLANNING YOUR ORGANIC FLOWER GARDEN

Also in this series

PLANNING YOUR ORGANIC VEGETABLE GARDEN
by Dick Kitto

PLANNING YOUR Organic

HERB GARDEN

SUE STICKLAND

Line illustrations by Nils Solberg
Herb drawings by Alison Ross

Thorsons
An Imprint of HarperCollins*Publishers*

Thorsons
An Imprint of HarperCollins*Publishers*
77–85 Fulham Palace Road,
Hammersmith, London W6 8JB

Published by Thorsons 1986
5   7   9   10   8   6

© Sue Stickland 1986

Sue Stickland asserts the moral right to
be identified as the author of this work

A catalogue record for this book
is available from the British Library

ISBN 0 7225 1143 4

Printed in Hong Kong

Cover shows The National Asthma Campaign Garden
designed by Lucy Huntington, Chelsea Flower Show 1993.
Photograph by John Glover/The Garden Picture Library.

CONTENTS

Chapter   *Page*

1. What is a Herb? — 9
2. Choosing Your Herbs — 11
3. Choosing the Site — 17
4. Designing the Herb Garden — 19
5. Preparing for Planting — 33
6. Propagating and Buying Plants — 37
7. Maintenance of the Herb Garden — 47
8. Harvesting and Preserving — 53
9. The Culinary Herb Garden — 61
10. Herb Teas and Drinks — 71
11. The Medicinal and Cosmetic Herb Garden — 73
12. The Pot-pourri Garden — 79
13. Herbs on the Patio — 85
14. Herbs Around the Garden — 89
15. Growing Information for Individual Herbs — 93

The Herb Gardening Calendar — 119
Further Reading — 121
Useful Addresses — 123
Index — 125

ACKNOWLEDGEMENTS

Many thanks to the following for letting me take photographs in their gardens as reference for the drawings and for the colour plates in this book:

Mr G. Acloque, Alderley Grange, Wootton-under-Edge, Glos; Joy Bramley; Mr and Mrs C. Dove; Sarah Garland; Mr D. Goodall; Judith and Simon Hopkinson, Hollington Nurseries, Woolton Hill, Newbury, Berks; Mr O. N. Menhinick, Lackham College of Agriculture, Nr Chippenham, Wilts; Mr R. Seelig; Mr and Mrs J. R. Sturgis; Rosemary Verey, Barnsley House, Nr Cirencester, Glos; Lorna and Rob Wild; Peter and Gilliam Wimperis, Selsey Herb Farm, Nr Stroud, Glos.

Also thanks to Helen Porter for help with the designs, to Mr and Mrs Stickland for help with typing, and to Mr and Mrs Goodall for help with the botany.

CHAPTER 1
WHAT IS A HERB?

Herbs are plants that are useful to us: mostly for their flavour, scent or medicinal properties, but sometimes in other ways about the house or garden.

Whatever you use them for, fresh herbs are far superior to dried herbs and those that you dry yourself are far better than the shop-bought versions. Luckily you don't need 'green fingers' or lots of space and time to grow them—they are generally undemanding but fascinating plants. This book concentrates on those that are most practical to grow and to use, whether or not you are familiar with herbs or with gardening—not forgetting, of course, that herbs can also be most attractive plants.

Another advantage of having your own herb garden is that the leaves you pick can be free from any harmful traces of pesticides or fertilizers. Growing herbs 'organically'—that is without chemicals—is by far the best method and is the one described throughout this book: it safeguards not only your health and that of your plants, but the whole ecology of your garden. In the organic garden, you encourage the growth of healthy plants and the presence of beneficial insects and micro-organisms which keep pests and diseases in check.

The uses of herbs
In cooking herbs are distinguished from vegetables in that relatively small amounts of the plant are used. Some are stronger than others: you need much smaller quantities of the pungent herbs basil or sweet marjoram, for example, than of parsley and chives (more about this in Chapter 9). There are also mild herbs like salad burnet and Good King Henry, needed in relatively large but still 'herbal' quantities: they are not highly bred like modern vegetable varieties and are concentrated sources of vitamins and minerals.

These health-giving elements are only part of the medicinal properties of herbs. Some herbal extracts still provide powerful drugs—for example, the heart drug digitalin comes from foxgloves. Such herbs as these are poisonous and must only be used by qualified herbalists so we will not be considering them in this book. However, there are many herbs which can be used by anyone to treat minor ailments at home. The remedies are simple yet wonderfully effective: the soothing effect of peppermint tea on the stomach or of comfrey leaves on cuts and bruises, for example. And there are no unpleasant side effects. A medicinal herb garden (such as that described in Chapter 11) can quickly become your alternative to the bathroom medicine cabinet.

It is hardly surprising that some of these herbs are also useful in cosmetics: for skin, hair, eyes and body. Apart from the scents that they impart, the health giving properties of the plants enhance their action. For example, some herbal bath mixtures have a relaxing effect as well as lovely smell.

Herbs are now used less around the house than they were before our modern household polishes, cleaners and dyes were available. Although it is possible to make these substances (and natural plant dyes in particular can outdo their chemical equivalents), the art is more for the enthusiast. However, capturing the scent of dried herbs in a fragrant *pot-pourri* or more pungent moth repellent, is something that everybody can do easily. *Pot-pourri* herbs also look very attractive in the herb garden as we shall see in Chapter 12.

Our flowers and vegetables can benefit as much as us from the effects of herbs. Grown amongst crops as 'companion' plants, their scent can deter insect pests; whilst various herbal brews can act as pesticides, fungicides or fertilizers. Thus they play an important part in organic growing. Herbs also attract large numbers of bees, butterflies and other useful insects. As well as benefitting fruit and vegetable crops, these all add to the delight of a herb garden on a sunny day!

The constituents of herbs
Since herbs can be effective in such small amounts, they obviously contain some powerful substances. The nature of these 'active' ingredients influences how the herbs should be grown and used, so it is worth knowing a bit about them.

Many herbs contain *volatile* or *aromatic oils*, which are some of the most important constituents as far as home herb growing is concerned: they are usually responsible for giving herbs their strong scent and most of them also act as antiseptics. A good example is the oil 'thymol' from thyme which is commonly employed in day-to-day items like toothpaste. The oils are contained within the tissues of the plant, their concentration depending on its stage of growth and the growing conditions. And, as the name indicates, they escape rapidly when the tissues are crushed; hence the need for proper harvesting and storing methods to capture the maximum possible scent and flavour.

As we have already seen, herbs also contain a wide range of *vitamins* and *minerals*, and these are in a form readily assimilated by the body. Some—like the vitamin C from parsley—are lost rapidly after the leaves are picked and even more are lost on cooking; hence the importance of having your own homegrown supply of fresh herbs and incorporating them regularly in your diet.

The other groups of substances commonly found in herbs have more bearing on their medicinal uses. The most familiar are *tannins* (as in tea) which have an astringent action, *bitters* which stimulate the digestive system (hence their use in aperitifs) and *mucilages* which are the slimy constituents of herbal remedies, and have a protective, soothing effect.

Less familiar and more complex in their effect are the *saponins, glycocides* and *alkaloids*. Herbs containing these substances are used to make powerful drugs, as mentioned earlier. The alkaloids in particular (like coniine from hemlock) can be poisonous unless used correctly, so these herbs are not ones to grow in the garden. Some home remedies do, however, employ herbs containing saponins and glycocides but these should be treated with caution.

An individual herb will often contain two or three of the active substances described here and it is the way these work together—one enhancing, cushioning or prolonging the action of the others—that makes herbs so valuable in the treatment of illness and in the diet.

CHAPTER 2
CHOOSING YOUR HERBS

This obviously depends on which herbs you like and will find most useful, but you must also consider what space you have to grow them, what the site is like and how much time you have to spend. If you have no ideas, start by looking at the designs in Chapters 9-12. See what is available in your local nursery or garden centre and, best of all, visit other gardens and see herbs growing.

There are several things you should find out about any herb that you plan to put in your garden: its correct name (this is not as silly or easy as it sounds!), whether it is annual or perennial, its manner of growth and the conditions it needs to grow well.

The naming of herbs

Some herbs have several different common names, which can be confusing: lovage is sometimes called 'love parsley', although it is certainly not a type of parsley, whilst southernwood is called 'lad's love' by some and 'old man' by others! Thus it is a good idea to become familiar with the Latin names of herbs—certainly before ordering plants by post from a catalogue. These names also give you some idea of what the herb is like.

Plants are grouped into botanical 'families' that have certain characteristics in common. The names of the families usually end in '-ae' and are often printed in plain type or capitals and put in brackets after the italicized name of

the plant. Thus parsley is *Petroselinum crispum* (Umbelliferae). Many other common herbs like fennel, dill, angelica and caraway belong to the Umbelliferae family: they all have flowers grouped into 'umbels' like flat-topped umbrellas (Figure 1a).

The other common herb family is Labiatae, which includes most of the remaining culinary herbs: mint, rosemary, sage, basil, thyme and marjoram. They all have flowers with a 'labiate' or lip which is helpful to visiting bees (Figure 1b).

The herb tarragon, together with chamomile and yarrow, belongs to the 'Compositae' family. This is the daisy family where tiny flowers are bunched into a 'composite' head (Figure 1c).

Thus knowing the family that a herb belongs to will often tell you something about its flower structure, which insects pollinate it, and sometimes to which pests and diseases it is prone. (It is not uncommon to see the leaves of horseradish stripped to a skeleton by cabbage-white butterflies: this is not so surprising when you find out that, like cabbages, it belongs to the Cruciferae family!)

The families are divided up into more closely related groups of plants or 'genera'. The 'genus' (singular) of a plant is indicated by the first part of its Latin name: 'Petroselinum' for parsley; 'Mentha' for all the different mints (peppermint, spearmint, etc.); 'Thymus' for all the different thymes. A plant's genus tells you quite a bit about it: for example all mints are likely to have creeping stems; all thymes are likely to have small, hard aromatic leaves.

Most of the genera are subdivided into 'species', giving the plants the second part of their Latin name, and these are often descriptive: *Mentha 'piperata'* for 'peppermint' and *Mentha 'rotundifolia'* for the 'round-leaved' apple mint. The description *'vulgaris'*, often encountered, simply means 'common' (as in *Thymus vulgaris* for the common garden thyme); that of *'officinalis'* is interesting—it means that the herb was once used for its medicinal properties.

Within the species there are often various 'varieties', and these have only small differences between them—perhaps just the colour or shape of the leaves or colour of the flowers. The inclusion of a multiplication sign indicates that the plant is a 'hybrid'—the result of crossing two species (and thus will not grow true from seed). For example, lemon thyme *Thymus × citriodora* is a cross between two *Thymus* species. In practice, however, the × is often omitted.

Annual and perennial herbs

Annual herbs are ones that germinate, grow, flower, set seed and die all in one year: in fact some herbs, like chervil, can have more than one generation per year. Other examples of annual herbs are dill, borage, rocket and summer savory.

Biennial herbs grow from seed to a leafy plant during one year; this lasts over winter and then flowers, sets seed and dies the next year (you will probably recognize that parsley behaves like this). More examples are given in Table 2 (page 15).

Sometimes annuals and biennials will

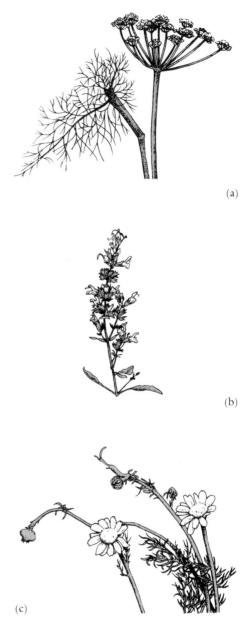

(a)

(b)

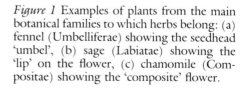

(c)

Figure 1 Examples of plants from the main botanical families to which herbs belong: (a) fennel (Umbelliferae) showing the seedhead 'umbel', (b) sage (Labiatae) showing the 'lip' on the flower, (c) chamomile (Compositae) showing the 'composite' flower.

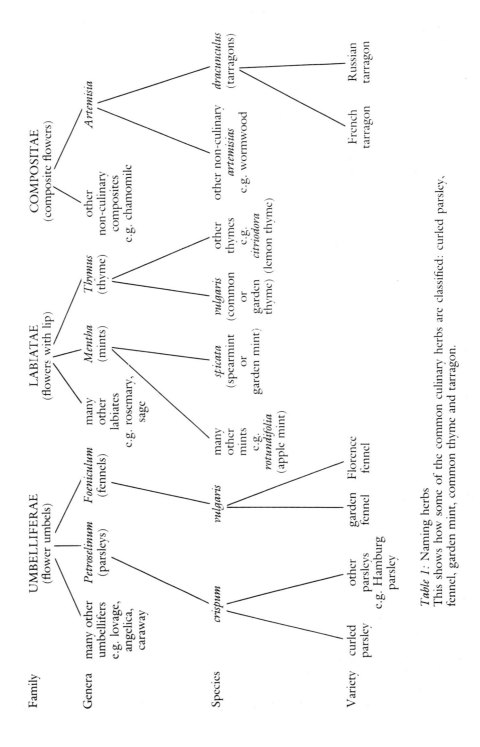

Table 1: Naming herbs
This shows how some of the common culinary herbs are classified: curled parsley, fennel, garden mint, common thyme and tarragon.

'self-seed': the seeds that they produce germinate where they fall, often all over the herb garden and elsewhere too, as anyone who has grown borage will know! Otherwise annuals and biennials must be sown every year to get a good continuous supply. Thus for these herbs it is generally better to buy a packet of seed than a plant from a nursery or garden centre, and you must be prepared for the trouble of sowing them and dealing with unwanted seedlings.

Perennial herbs, on the other hand, will grow on from one year to the next. Some are relatively short lived: angelica, for example, may only live three or four years (cutting off the flowerhead in its early stages is said to prolong the life of the plant, but this seems a shame as it is so handsome). Other perennial herbs will last for ten years or more, although sometimes younger plants look better and have a better flavour; thus a gradual renewal programme (as described on page 52) is a good idea for an established garden.

Herbaceous and shrubby herbs
Some perennial herbs are 'herbaceous'—that is, they die down completely in winter; you may even have to mark their positions with sticks so that you can identify the young shoots quickly in the spring. You should find out the height of any herb you are thinking of growing. Angelica can tower above you when it is in flower, which seems impossible when buying the plant a few inches high. Similarly lovage can reach over five feet. Some of these tall plants can be grown in a small garden, but you have to be rigorous about controlling them as we shall see in Chapter 7. Otherwise they are very little trouble to grow.

Other perennial herbs are 'shrubby', keeping a woody framework from year to year. They vary from full-size garden shrubs like elder, which easily reaches twelve feet or more, to small compact ones like garden thyme, which grows about a foot high; there are even tiny creeping thymes about an inch high which are ideal for putting between paving stones. Again it is essential to find out the final height of any shrubby herb you intend to grow. Most of them keep their leaves throughout the winter, although some, like hyssop, will become bare if the winter is severe.

Hardy and half-hardy herbs
The easiest herbs to grow are those which are 'hardy: that is, they can survive out of doors all year round. This depends partly on where you live: lemon verbena might be considered hardy on the South coast, but elsewhere it would need taking into a greenhouse or conservatory in winter. Rosemary is generally hardy in the South but would need protection in severe weather in the North. Sometimes cold wet springs rather than severe winter frosts take most toll of the shrubby Mediterranean herbs like winter savory and lemon thyme.

'Hardy annual' herbs are those that can be sown directly outside (like borage and chervil) and, as we have seen, they often seed themselves once they are established. 'Half-hardy annuals', however, must be sown in pots indoors and then planted out; this is because the seeds need a higher temperature to germinate and the plants need extra warmth to develop. If we waited for the temperature outside to reach the required levels, these herbs would not have time to grow properly before the autumn.

Thus of all the types of herb, half-hardy annuals are the most trouble to grow. Nevertheless, some of them have such distinct and pleasantly pungent flavours that the effort is well

Table 2: Annual and biennial herbs

Hardy annuals	Half-hardy annuals (or grown as such)	Hardy biennials
Borage	Sweet basil	Caraway
Chervil	Bush basil	Evening primrose
Coriander	Purple basil	Mullein
Dill	Lemon bergamot	Parsley
German chamomile	Sweet marjoram	Woad
Lamb's lettuce		
Nasturtium		
Pot marigold		
Purslane		
Rocket		
Summer savory		

worthwhile: basil is probably the most familiar example. Chapter 6 describes how you can grow such herbs successfully, even without a greenhouse.

Sun-loving and moisture-loving herbs

Many herbs will grow tolerably well in a range of conditions, but some have special needs: one may need full sun and dry soil and another shade and moist soil in order to flourish. Remember that our herb gardens are probably far removed from the plant's natural habitat. For example, many of what we consider common culinary herbs like rosemary, sage and thyme would not have been available to our pre-Roman ancestors; their 'pot' herbs would have been plants like nettles, dandelion, mugwort and comfrey. The Romans brought over two hundred herbs to Britain—and many of these would be more at home on a dry Mediterranean hillside. Other herbs like bergamot and lemon verbena were introduced from America after the first settlers learnt about them from the Indians. On the other hand many cultivated mints have the wild water mint in their ancestry: they thus grow best in damp places and rarely thrive in dry ones. Other herbs which like moist soil and partial shade are angelica, bergamot, comfrey, meadowsweet and sweet cicely.

Thus it is worth finding out the conditions which best suit any herb you are thinking of growing. More guidance on this is given in Chapter 3.

CHAPTER 3
CHOOSING THE SITE

The questions you should ask yourself when considering a site for a herb garden are:

Is it sunny?
Is it sheltered?
How well does it drain?
What is the soil like?
How accessible is it?

Sunshine

At least part of your site should face south, for growing the aromatic sun-loving herbs like rosemary, savory and thyme. This is the factor which should most influence your choice, because shelter, soil and drainage are easier to improve.

Although these Mediterranean herbs may *survive* in damper, shadier places, they really need sunshine to concentrate the aromatic oils and bring out their full fragrance and flavour. There are, of course, herbs such as parsley and mint which will tolerate a little shade, and yet others like sorrel and sweet cicely which will grow well in partial or dappled shade.

Shelter

This is also important for a herb garden: cold spring winds can do more harm to tender herbs than very low temperatures, and in summer a windy site means more work staking up the taller herbs. It is not only the plants that appreciate a sheltered site: the many butterflies and bees that herbs attract will not come if it is too windswept, and for us too the herb garden should be an enjoyable place to sit in the summer.

Thus a site which already has house or garden walls to the north and east is ideal, but you can provide some shelter if necessary by putting up low walls or fences or by growing herb hedges (see pages 24-27).

Drainage

As could be expected from their Mediterranean origin, the one thing the many aromatic herbs dislike above all else is having 'wet feet'. Thus the greater part of your site must be well drained. One slightly sloping to the south would be ideal, and one that could become very waterlogged is best avoided completely. Between these two extremes you can compromise: first by trying to improve the drainage and second by setting aside wetter areas for the moisture-loving herbs.

Often drainage can be greatly improved simply by forking over the soil to two-spades depth: this will break up any compacted layers just beneath the surface. However, you may need to make a soakaway. To do this dig a hole about 3 feet (0.9m) deep and 2 feet (0.6m) square, fill it two-thirds full with broken bricks, stones and gravel, and replace the top soil.

Alternatively you can avoid the problem by making raised beds, as described on page 26.

Soil

A light, slightly alkaline soil is best for most herbs: a heavy clay soil tends to become waterlogged and a very rich soil causes the herbs to make lush growth in which the aromatic oils are less concentrated. Most soils, whether too poor or too heavy, can be improved with the right treatment but you should consider the time and effort involved in this when choosing a site. It is easy to test the acidity of the soil using one of the cheap 'pH' test kits on the market. Although the pH level is not critical for growing herbs, many are native to alkaline territory—chalk downs and limestone hills. Thus it is advisable to add lime to acid soils to bring the pH to 7 or just above by following the instructions in the kit.

Accessibility

The most convenient place to have a herb garden is usually outside the kitchen door. On the other hand, there is no point in trying to make one here if conditions are not right. If your nearest suitable site is right down the garden then that is where your herbs should be. But you could also grow some of your much-used favourites in pots on a patio or even on the kitchen window sill (see Chapter 13).

CHAPTER 4
DESIGNING THE HERB GARDEN

This is the most exciting part—trying to visualize what your herb garden could look like and getting a realistic design. You must match your ideas with the constraints of your site and the materials, time and expertise available.

As we shall see in this chapter, access paths are one of the most important parts of the design even in a small garden. Then you must think of the boundaries: walls, fences, and herb hedges. Perhaps you might like a scented arbour, a sundial or a seat from which to appreciate the magical qualities of your garden—the smells and the flowers, the butterflies and bees it attracts. You must also consider the best positions for the herbs you have chosen, and which herbs best fit the empty spaces on your plan—the awkward shady corners or the sides of a bank. A well thought out design will make your herb garden a success right from the start.

Measuring the site
It is best to make a plan on paper first—where it is easier to draw and rub out lines and fit curves. This also helps you to overcome preconceived ideas based on what the site looks like now, and thus to explore completely new possibilities.

Start by making a simple sketch plan of the site, marking the boundaries and main fixtures (buildings, walls, trees which must be kept, etc.) and distances between them. Don't use graph paper at this stage: what first appear to be right angles and straight boundaries often turn out to be far from square; in particular the depth of corners is deceptive. If your site is large and irregular in shape you can measure it accurately by using two sets of bamboo canes as shown in Figure 2.

Now make an accurate plan from your sketch and measurements—draw bold outlines and use overlays of tracing paper to try out different designs.

Paths and stepping stones
The plants in a herb garden are continually being picked for use and ideally you should be able to reach all of them without getting muddy feet.

This is possible in a long narrow border, one or two plants deep: and such a border makes a very functional herb garden especially if it is outside the kitchen door. A slightly wider border may need occasional 'stepping stones'—made from paving slabs, three or four bricks laid together or irregular flat stones (Figure 3). On a larger plot you will need many more 'steps' or plenty of paths.

One classic design is a chequerboard of square paving slabs with herbs planted in every other square (Figure 4a). This is very attractive for a formal garden: the herbs are easily accessible and, if only one type is put in each space, they are easily kept in hand.

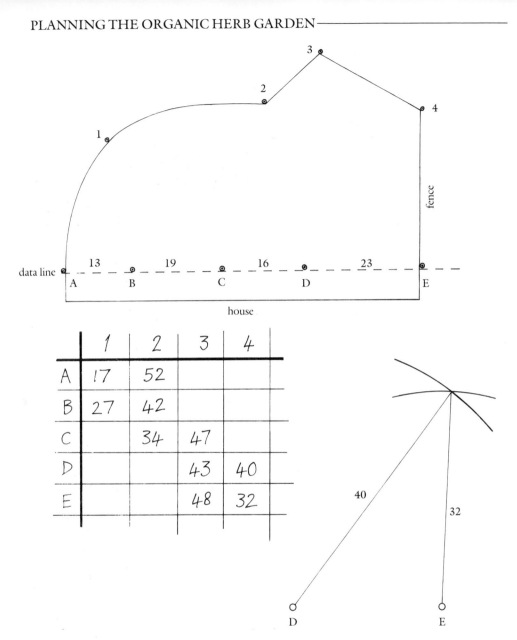

Figure 2 Measuring the site:

1. Lay down a straight data line with bamboo canes A, B, C, D etc. across an accessible part of the garden and measure the distances between them;

2. Mark relevant points on the boundary of the site with another set of canes 1, 2, 3, 4, etc.;

3. Measure the distance of each point from two of the canes (using a tape measure or by pacing) and record the results in a table;

4. Use a pair of compasses to mark out the points on plain paper and hence draw your outline.

Figure 3 Stepping stones in a narrow border
to make all the herbs easily accessible.

However, it does take up a lot of space and the paving stones can be expensive. You can adapt the design, of course, and have far fewer slabs. Alternatively, on an existing patio just remove odd squares here and there for planting.

Before deciding on such a design, check what sort of slabs are available locally: most big garden centres stock a range of concrete slabs in a variety of colours usually from one to two feet square (0.3 × 0.3 m^2 to 0.6× 0.6 m^2) but also in rectangular and hexagonal shapes. For a large number you would be best to go to a builder's merchant or check the local paper. Reconstituted stone slabs are nicer but more expensive, and in some areas you may be able to get hold of natural stone slabs—at a price!

The other classic design which gives maximum accessibility to all the herbs is the 'cart-wheel', where paths form the spokes and the beds are the areas between them (Figure 4b). Paths in concentric circles also work well as does a combination of the two designs (Figures 4c and 4d).

The most adaptable design is probably a geometric arrangement of rectangular beds; remember you must be able to reach all the herbs, so these beds should not be more than 4 feet (1.2 m) wide (Figure 4e).

Paths can be laid to grass or made of gravel, bricks, blocks or paving slabs. The disadvantage of grass paths is that they have to be mown and edged, thus they are only feasible in a large herb garden; however they look attractive and restful, and show off the herbs well. A gravel path is simple to lay and looks good but its problem is weeds—and there is no easy organic answer to this one. The alternatives (bricks, blocks, etc.) require cement and mortar and you may find this daunting. However, it can be done a little at a time—on short brick paths you could even introduce a pattern—and it can be a pleasing task.

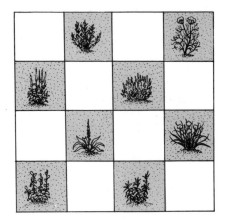

A

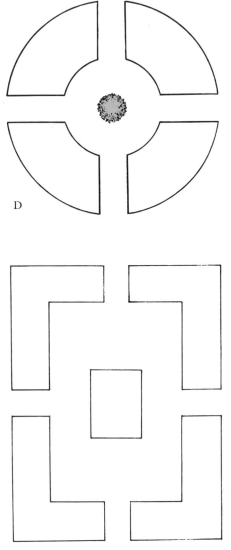

D

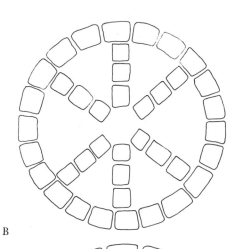

B

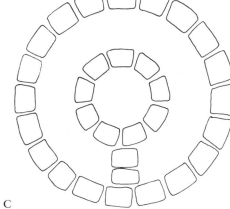

C

E

Figure 4 Simple herb garden designs which make all the herbs accessible from paths or stepping stones: (a) chequerboard; (b) cart-wheel; (c) concentric circles; (d) quadrants; (e) geometric patterns of rectangular beds.

Low creeping herbs can be used to fill gaps between irregular paving or larger areas between stepping stones. The idea that their scent wafts up as you walk on them is a nice one, but does not always work in practice. However they are very attractive and add to the fascination of the herb garden. Most effective are the many and varied creeping thymes: the flowers of the different varieties range from white to deep purple and the foliage from dark and furry to light and fresh. Some of the most widely available varieties do not smell strongly and some do not lie as flat as others (see Table 3), so it is worth studying the catalogues carefully. On the other hand, the tiny creeping Corsican mint *(Mentha requienii)* covers the ground like moss and has an incredibly strong peppermint smell, out of all proportion to its size! It does best in shady places. Lawn or

'Treneague' chamomile is the favourite herb for covering large areas—it is a low-growing perennial chamomile which does not flower.

Sometimes it is an advantage to choose a creeping herb that is easy to propagate: the more plants you have to start with, the quicker the area is covered. (Wild creeping thyme *Thymus serpyllum,* for example, can be grown easily from seed.) You should aim to put all these creeping plants not more than 6 inches (15 cm) apart.

Walls and fences

As we have already seen, a herb garden should be sheltered, ideally making use of existing house and garden walls and boundary fences. These can be used to support climbers appropriate to the herb garden (see Table 4) which will also disguise them if necessary. Scented

Table 3: Creeping herbs

Herb	Height	Appearance and scent	Other comments
Thymes			
Thymus serpyllum (wild thyme)	1½in (3cm)	Dark green leaves, pink flowers, faint thyme-like smell.	Hardy, can be grown from seed. Unnamed catalogue varieties are likely to be this one.
Thymus serpyllum albus	1½in (3cm)	Light green leaves, white flowers	
Thymus serpyllum lanuginosus	1½in (3cm)	Grey/green woolly leaves, pink flowers	
Thymus herba barona	1½in (3cm)	Dark leaves, deep pink flowers, caraway scent.	All the creeping thymes thrive in dry sunny places.
Thymus 'Doone valley'	3in (7.5cm)	Variegated gold/green leaves, lemon scent.	
Mints			
Mentha requienii (Corsican mint)	½in (1cm)	Tiny leaves and purple flowers, very strong peppermint scent.	Prefers partially shaded moist places; may need some nurturing.
Mentha pulegium (creeping pennyroyal)	4in (10cm)	Bright green leaves, purple flowers, sweet peppermint scent.	Needs good moist soil.
Chamomile			
Anthemis nobilis 'Treneague' (lawn chamomile)	1in (2.5cm)	Non-flowering chamomile, sweet scent.	Tolerates fairly dry situations.

Figure 5 Intertwining box hedges forming a 'knot garden'.

roses, for example, are never out of place and for most positions in the garden you should be able to find a variety that will do well. Those in the table are all fairly disease-resistant (an important consideration for the organic gardener), but there are many more that are suitable.

Alternatively you might consider building a low wall of brick or stone round the herb garden—or at least on the exposed north and east sides of it. The creeping thymes described for paths would grow equally well in large earth-filled crevices in a dry stone wall. Or leave a deeper gap on top of the wall—say 10 inches wide by 4 inches deep (25 cm × 10 cm)—and fill it with compost and soil. Other low growing aromatic herbs which like dry conditions, such as wall germander and dwarf lavender, will flourish here.

Hedges and edges

Although they do provide shelter, ordinary garden hedges make less suitable surrounds to a herb garden than walls. They will all deplete the soil near to them (privet worse than most) and yew, in particular, should be avoided as its spiky leaves are highly poisonous.

Large, loose hedges do not show herbs off to their best advantage. However, closely clipped box hedges are traditional in the herb garden—as much for show as for shelter. They were often used in the Elizabeth 'knot gardens': intertwining, looping patterns of low neat hedges on a gravel surface. Examples of 'knots' of varying complexity can be seen in many grand country house gardens today (Figure 5). A simple design like that in Figure 6 could be used as an outline for a small neat herb garden, where different herbs are planted in the loops.

Some herbs themselves will make attractive hedges (Table 5). Lavender, of course, is the most familiar. Old English lavender will grow to about 3 feet (1 metre) and provide some shelter as well as a lasting display of highly coloured and scented flowers; a long hedge of this can be very striking. Rosemary bushes will form a similar hedge, but this itself needs a sheltered position and you should only consider it if you live in Southern England: losing a hedge in a hard winter leaves a more noticeable gap than any loss of single plants.

Several herbs are suitable for low hedges in a herb garden, as part of the

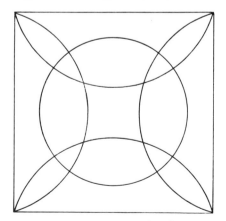

Figure 6 A simple knot garden design.

Table 4: Climbing herbs for walls, fences, arbours and arches.

Climber	Height	Description	Comment
Roses			
'Compassion'	8ft (2.4m)	Pink/apricot flowers, very fragrant	Suitable for walls and arches.
'Dublin bay'	8ft (2.4m)	Double, brilliant deep red flowers throughout season	Moderately vigorous, good for small arbours.
'Schoolgirl'	10–12ft (3.0–3.6m)	Orange/apricot double flowers, sweetly scented, summer through to autumn.	Moderately vigorous. Good for west wall.
'Mme Alfred Carriére'	15–20ft (4.5–6.0m)	White flush pink double flowers, recurrently to autumn.	Vigorous if in full sun. Will grow on north wall.
Hops			
Humulus lupulus	20ft (6m)	Pale green, vine-shaped leaves. Papery cone-shaped flowers.	Suitable for arbours in sunny places. Need rich soil.
Vine			
Vitus vinifera (wine grape)	20ft (6m)	Typical lobed fresh green leaves, colouring in autumn when grapes are produced.	Ornamental varieties like 'Brandt', 'apiifolia' are available and very suitable for covering an arbour, but could also be grown on wires on a wall.
Blackberry			
Rubus fruticosus e.g. 'Oregon thornless'	6–8ft (1.8–2.4m)	Deeply cut attractive leaves, large sweet fruit in September/October	On walls in sun or partial shade. Best in moisture retentive soil.
Honeysuckle			
Lonicera periclymenum	15–20ft (4.5–6m)	The traditional native honeysuckle. Flowers July and August.	Best on well-drained soil in light shade.

design rather than to perform any function. Dwarf varieties of lavender are more compact than the Old English but equally attractive; hyssop makes a similar flowering hedge or it can be closely clipped. One of the quickest to form a dense hedge is cotton lavender—it can be kept pleasingly neat and square if cut regularly.

Spacing of the plants does depend partly on the variety (see Table 5); the closer together you put them, however, the quicker you get a complete hedge. Again it is an advantage to be able to propagate the plants yourself.

Herb hedges are ideal for a large formal herb garden, but in other situations they may not be worth the space: they need regular attention and, with the possible exception of lavender, the large quantities of leaves and flowers they produce cannot be used.

In small gardens it may be better to use naturally low-growing, bushy herbs to edge the beds: perhaps a row of parsley, chives or salad burnet, or a mixture of two of them. It is an ideal role for herbs that you use a lot. Other examples are given in Table 6.

Raised beds

Raised beds are particularly useful on a poorly drained site; they also add variety of height to the garden and bring fragrant herbs nearer to nose level! They can be anything from about 1 foot to 2 feet 6 inches high (0.3 to 0.75 m), and should not be more than about 4 feet (1.2 m) wide as you must be able to reach the middle easily.

The beds can be contained by walls of brick or stone, planks of treated timber, or old railway sleepers. High beds need proper walls with concrete foundations because they have to withstand considerable pressure from the soil. They are thus a major task. However, much lower beds—easier to construct—can

still improve drainage considerably. In an informal setting, planks laid on edge and held with pegs driven in on either side look acceptable, particularly when partly disguised by overhanging edging herbs.

If drainage is bad, lay a 6-inch (15 cm) layer of hardcore or gravel between the walls of high raised beds before filling them up with a mixture of good soil, compost, peat and sharp sand. With low beds, fork over the soil beneath before raising them with the same mixture.

Seats and scented arbours

A herb garden, sunny and sheltered, is just the place to sit and relax. In a large garden a seat could be a central feature or could be situated in a concealed spot at the end of one of the paths. Do not dismiss the idea for a small garden either: herbs can be grown round a seat, under it, over it and even on top of it, so it need not deprive you of much planting space!

Traditional 'herb seats' consisted of cushions of creeping herbs let into a bank or wall. However, in our climate these would so often be too damp to sit on that it is more practical to make the top from large flat stones with creeping herbs between them. Alternatively, a free-standing wooden garden seat or bench could be used with soft, flowing herbs like the sweet-smelling mints, lemon balm and scented geraniums growing around it.

The seat can feel even more secretive and magical if it is under an arbour of climbing plants. Such arbours are usually made of wood: either 'rustic' poles or squared lengths of timber. Be generous in the thickness, allowing at least 3 inches (7.5 cm) and set the uprights well into the ground, as the structure will have to bear a considerable weight of foliage. To help the climbers to clothe the arbour you will need hori-

Table 5: Hedging herbs

Herb	Height	Description	Distance between plants	Comment
Old English Lavender *Lavandula spica*	2ft (60cm)	Loose hedge, classic purple flowers	18–24in (45–60cm)	Hardy and will tolerate dry conditions. Sunny position. Can be grown from seed.
Hidcote Lavender *Lavandula spica*	18in (45cm)	Loose hedge, dark purple flowers	18–24in (45–60cm)	Hardy and tolerates dry conditions. Sunny position.
Lavender 'Munstead dwarf' *Lavandula vera*	12in (30cm)	Compact hedge, purple flowers	12–18in (30–45cm)	Hardy and tolerates dry conditions. Sunny position. Can be grown from seed.
Rosemary (common) *Rosmarinus officinalis*	3ft (1m)	Loose flowering grey green hedge, blue flowers	18–24in (45–60cm)	Needs a sunny sheltered position. Propagates fairly easily from cuttings.
Rosemary 'Mrs Jessups Upright' *Rosmarinus officinalis*	3ft (1m)	Thicker, more formal hedge	18–24in (45–60cm)	Needs a sunny sheltered position. Propagates fairly easily from cuttings. The hardiest variety.
Cotton lavender *Santolina chamaecyparissus*	2ft (60cm)	Silver grey foliage, dense hedge	18–24in (45–60cm)	Hardy and dependable. Grows quickly. Propagates easily from cuttings.
Winter savory *Satureia montana*	12in (30cm)	Mid-green foliage. White flowers	12in (30cm)	Fairly hardy although may lose some leaves in winter. Tolerates dry conditions. Sunny position. Grows easily from seed.
Hyssop *Hyssopus officinalis*	20in (50cm)	Dark green foliage. Blue, pink or white flowers, if not vigorously clipped	18in (45cm)	Sunny position. May lose leaves in hard winter. Can grow from seed.
Wall germander *Teucrium chamaedrys*	18in (45cm)	Dark shiny scolloped leaves, pink flowers	12in (30cm)	Relatively slow growing. Will propagate from cuttings, but not readily. Tolerates dry conditions.
Southernwood *Artemisia abrotanum*	3ft (1m)	Feathery green leaves	18–24in (45–60cm)	Sunny position. Needs hard clipping. Propagates from cuttings.
Curry plant *Helichrysum angustifolium*	2ft (60cm)	Silver foliage, dense hedge	18in (45cm)	Sunny position. Propagates easily from cuttings.

zontal struts or wires about 20 inches (0.5 m) apart.

Hops are one of the most useful herbal climbers for arbours: they have a reputation for inducing sleep and are a valuable medicinal herb. Their pale green, vine-like leaves and loose clusters of flower 'cones' make them an attractive candidate (Figure 7). Scented climbing roses of moderate vigour are the other obvious choice, perhaps combined with an outdoor vine (see Table 4).

Features and focal points
Eye-catching statues and sundials are a feature of many formal herb gardens, adding to the fascination of the design.

Figure 7 Hops climb vigorously over the wooden framework of an arbour.

In the 'cart-wheel' layout (page 21), the obvious focal point is the central pivot. The end of a path is also a good position in designs, and will most draw the idle wanderer down to it. Other formal features include urns of trailing herbs and clipped bay trees.

Some of these ideas can be adapted to provide points of interest in small, less formal gardens without necessarily involving alot of expense. For example, you could use an old sink to plant out the half-hardy scented geraniums. Similarly allocate space for a bay tree or lemon verbena plant which has been inside during the winter—use a large terracotta pot or a wooden tub. A strawberry pot is a good home for creeping thymes. We will be looking at herbs in pots in detail in Chapter 13.

A small pool can add considerable interest to the herb garden, and a marshy area is an environment that suits many useful herbs. Formal gardens usually have a geometrically shaped pool with a paved surround, occasionally with a modest fountain. The best pool depth is about 2 feet (60cm), with a planting shelf around the edge (9 inches (23cm) below the surface for appropriate 'marginal' water plants like yellow flag *(Iris pseudacorus)*. Other herbs which could be included are brooklime *(Veronica beccabunga)*, bog-bean *(Menyanthes trifoliata)*, and watercress. Such formal pools could be made of concrete, but the special flexible liners now widely available are more satisfasctory. Pre-formed glass-fibre shapes make it even easier to 'do-it-yourself', if you can find one of a suitable shape and size.

In an informal garden, a small deep pool supplying a surrounding boggy area with water is the most useful. This provides ideal conditions for waterside plants like comfrey, meadowsweet and sweet cicely. Such a pool is best created with a flexible liner, but on a small scale improvising with sunken containers

Figure 8 An angelica plant with its handsome flower umbels can soon grow up to 6 feet (2m) tall.

Table 6: Edging herbs

Herb	Height	Description	Comment
Parsley *Petroselinum crispum* (curly-leaved varieties)	8in (20cm)	Bright green attractive foliage	Biennial—grows from seed but sometimes difficult to germinate. Needs rich soil to thrive; full sun or some shade.
Chives *Allium schoenoprasum*	6–12in (15–30cm)	Dense tufts, pink flowers	Perennial. Easy to propagate by seed or division. Prefers moist rich soil; full sun or some shade. Height depends on conditions and variety.
Salad burnet *Sanguisorba minor*	6–12in (15–30cm)	Dark green fern-like foliage	Perennial. Can be grown easily from seed. Tolerates most conditions.
Alpine strawberry *Fragaria vesca* (e.g. 'Alexandria', 'Baron Solemacher')	12in (30cm)	Sweet fruit (larger than wild strawberry) from July to October	Perennial. Can be grown easily from seed. Needs rich moist soil, sun or partial shade.
Dwarf nasturtiums *Trapeaolum majus* (e.g. Empress of India)	6–9in (15–22cm)	Large round leaves, scarlet/orange flowers	Annual. Grows easily from seed. Best on poor soil.
Heartsease pansies *Viola tricolor*	6in (15cm)	Tiny purple and yellow flowers	Perennial. Grows easily from seed.

kept regularly topped up with water can help along these moisture-loving plants.

Placing the herbs

When you have some idea of your basic design—paths, walls and other features—it is time to think about fitting in the herbs you have chosen and deciding what others are suitable for your site.

Some herb gardens have a theme for each of the various beds: an obvious choice is to divide culinary herbs from medicinal herbs and herbs used for their colour or fragrance. This is the division used in the designs in Chapters 9 to 12, but it is only an arbitrary one: many culinary herbs have medicinal properties and indeed were often used in cooking for precisely this reason—sage for example, was used with rich meats because it helps the digestion. Other themes might be a 'bee garden' to include those herbs most attractive to bees and butterflies, or a 'dyer's garden', a bed of herbs used for natural dyes. There are even gardens of Shakespearean herbs—those mentioned in his plays! Of course, you don't have to make divisions of this sort: mixing the herbs whatever their use is certainly more practical for a small plot. Either way, in placing the herbs you must consider

Table 7: Tall herbaceous perennial herbs

Herb	Height	Comment
Angelica *Angelica archangelica*	6ft (2m)	Attractive flower umbels on tall strong stems
Chicory *Cicorium intybus*	4ft (1.25m)	Blue flowers up tall stems which usually need staking
Comfrey *Symphytum officinale*	3ft (1m)	Generally floppy growth, keep trimmed
Elecampane *Inula helenium*	6ft (2m)	Huge leaves and yellow flowers, needs a lot of room
Fennel *Foeniculum vulgare*	5ft (1.5m)	Stiff upright growth, should not need staking
Lovage *Levisticum officinalis*	6ft (2m)	Strong upright growth but may need staking
Mullein *Verbascum thapsus*	3ft (1m)	Yellow flowers up strong flower spike
Sorrel, garden *Rumex acetosa*	2½ft (75cm)	Tall flower stems, but these are often removed
Tarragon, Russian *Artemisia dracunculus*	3ft (1m)	Floppy growth, needs staking

factors like how large they grow, whether they are annual or perennial, and what conditions they like.

There are a number of herbs which do grow very large (Table 7, Figure 8), and remember first appearances can be deceptive. However, a herb garden is not like an ordinary flower garden in that it is mostly fresh young leaves that are required. So some of the tall herbaceous herbs like fennel and lovage which grow up from clumps can still be accommodated in a small garden: keep them cut back and new growth will be produced at the base. On a larger plot, however, such tall herbs should be allowed to grow up and flower; place them at the back of a border or the centre of an island bed where they will not overshadow smaller plants. The taller herbs need plenty of space round them too—allow about 2 feet (0.6 m) between the herbs listed in Table 7.

Between these giants and the edging herbs discussed on pages 24 and 26 you can plant the moderate bushy herbs like sage and rosemary. If you have grown the plants yourself and have several of any one kind, you can put these out as a group about 1 foot (0.3 m) apart to give a quicker bushy effect. The extra plants could be removed in a year or two, but in general this will not be necessary. Shrubs like elder and raspberry which have a herbal use are often planted outside the main beds to fill in odd corners of the garden.

In the first year of the herb garden,

annuals can easily be sown or planted out in the spaces between perennials. After this, however, it becomes more difficult: the established herbs grow up quickly in spring and tend to overshadow seedlings and young plants. Thus annuals should be allocated open positions near the edges of beds if possible. In some designs they are given a bed of their own which is cleared and dug over each winter.

Try to give each herb its ideal growing conditions as far as possible: this is the key to having a healthy, successful garden. Aromatic herbs become rank and flavourless if grown in a damp shady corner, where mint on the other hand, would thrive. Some guidelines are given on pages 14-15, and more detail about individual herbs in Chapter 15.

A 'chequerboard' of paving slabs which gives good access to all the herbs.

Colourful compact nasturtiums make a useful edging to a bed of salad herbs—their leaves and flowers are edible.

The deep purple flowers of 'Hidcote' lavender.

A formal herb garden surrounded by low walls for shelter and laid out with gravel paths; a bay tree in a pot forms the central feature.

CHAPTER 5
PREPARING FOR PLANTING

With a design in hand, it is tempting to rush ahead and start planting. However, the importance of preparing the site well cannot be stressed enough: it will make all the difference to the health and success of the garden, saving you endless time later in weeding and nurturing plants.

Eliminating weeds
It is essential to get rid of all perennial weeds before planting. This advice is often given and equally often ignored but the effort is really worthy while. It is impossible to eliminate weeds like bindweed, couch grass and ground elder once they are growing up in amongst herbaceous plants. You will waste a lot of time weeding and, unless you are very vigilant, they will spread throughout the plot. If you know your site is badly infested, do not expect to be able to clear it in one go during the winter: it will take at least a month during the growing season and probably longer.

Weeds with tap roots like dandelion and docks can be lifted out with a spade—although if you break off the root below the surface it will resprout, and you will need to attack it several times until its energies are exhausted. Couch grass and ground elder can generally be forked out as long as your soil is not too heavy, but again you will need several attempts. However, if the roots form a solid mass you are in more trouble. Continually chopping them up—or even rotavating a large area—during a dry period in spring or summer and then raking up the loose roots can go a long way towards eliminating them.

The deeper roots of bindweed, creeping thistle and the tough spiky 'horsetail' make these weeds the most difficult to eradicate: the roots can go down 2 feet (0.6 m) or more and are almost impossible to dig out completely. (Horsetail, incidentally, is a weed associated with badly drained land, so you should take its appearance as a warning when looking for a herb garden site.) Moreover, these weeds do not emerge until very late spring so that it is often May before you realize the extent of the problem.

One sure method of killing them which involves no chemicals is to cover the whole plot with black plastic in the spring, and leave it down for a whole growing season. Dig a shallow trench round the area and bury the sides of the plastic in it; the wind will not then be able to lift it, and no shoots can force their way through—which they will do given half a chance! Starved of light and hence food, the leaves and the roots will have given up by the autumn. A thick newspaper mulch can similarly be effective, particularly against the shallower rooted perennials like couch and creeping buttercup. The difficulty is holding the papers down completely: using stones is time-consuming and does not always work. Covering the papers with a 6-inch (15 cm) layer of damp straw is a possibility and looks more in keeping with the garden.

Although there are no 'organic' weedkillers, the chemical ammonium sulphamate which is effective against most perennials could be considered as a last resort: it does less harm to the environment (and us!) than many of the modern weedkillers. It is marketed to amateur gardeners as white crystals which must be dissolved in water and sprayed on. It is taken in both by the leaves of weeds and their roots and therefore must not be used near plants or shrubs that you want to keep. The effect is noticeable within about a week but it is not safe to replant within two months of spraying (three months in dry weather), so again the eradication process is not a quick one. During this time, the ammonium sulphamate breaks down into ammonium sulphate which—while not exactly desirable in the organic garden—is a chemical which many gardeners apply as a fertilizer.

Marking out the design

If you are laying brick, stone or gravel paths, or sowing grass ones, these should be marked out using pegs and string before you go on to prepare the beds (see Figure 9). For a design with simple stepping stones, the whole area should be prepared as described in the next section before laying the stones.

Preparing the ground

The importance of good drainage in a herb garden means that you should dig the site as deeply as possible (see Figure 10). Even apparently good soil becomes compacted at lower levels and breaking up this compaction can have a lasting beneficial effect.

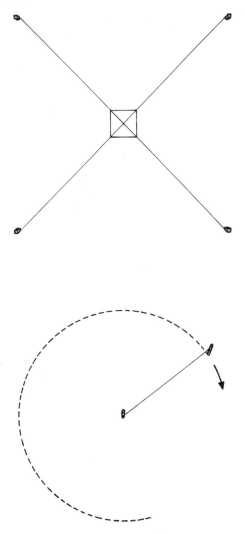

Figure 9 Marking out accurate squares and circles: the diagonals of the square are determined by the small square of cardboard in the centre. The circle outline can be marked by making a line in the earth or with a flexible hose-pipe.

You can tell how rich your soil is—that is, how high a level of plant nutrients it contains—by the general vigour of vegetable crops and newly established ornamental plants in your garden. Light sandy and silty soils tend to be deficient, whereas clay soils and loams are usually rich. If your soil is poor, you should incorporate some well-rotted manure or garden compost at this stage. If you only have a very small plot and find manure or compost difficult to obtain, then you could buy one of the proprietary dried manures that are often on sale in plastic sacks in garden centres. These are good but expensive for a large area. A heavy clay soil does not need extra nutrients, but will benefit from a similar addition of leafmould (or peat for a small area). This will help lighten the soil and prevent waterlogging of the plant roots.

A plot prepared in this way should suit most herbs: artificial fertilizers should not be used as they cause unwanted lush growth. However, extra compost or manure can be added in the planting holes for herbs like mint or chives which thrive on rich ground. Mint is notorious for its spreading roots which find their way into other plants, under fences and between paving stones! One solution is to contain them in large pots, old sinks, etc. around the herb garden, but this means frequent watering if they are to thrive. A better idea is to sink a bucket with holes in the bottom into the ground and fill it with a mixture of compost, peat and good garden soil; alternatively use a large heavy-duty polythene bag such as the bottom half of an old peat bag (see Figure 11).

The best time for preparing a site on heavy soil is early winter because frost can then break down the clods of earth before planting begins. On light soils early spring is better because they do not need to be weathered and the nutrients in the compost are not then washed out by winter rains.

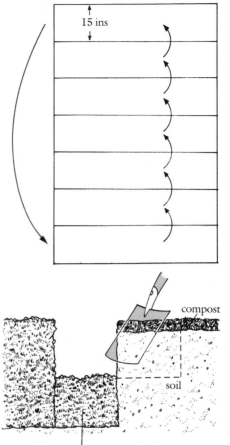

Figure 10 Deep digging the site: this method breaks up the soil and mixes in compost to two spades depth, to benefit both deep and shallow rooting herbs.

1. Spread compost over the surface of the plot.

2. Take out a trench about one spade's depth and 15 inches (40cm) wide across the plot, putting the soil in a barrow or on a plastic sheet.

3. Fork over the soil in the bottom of the trench, mixing it with extra compost.

4. Fill the trench with soil from the next 15 inches (40cm) strip, roughly mixing it with the compost on the surface.

5. Continue to the end of the plot, filling the last trench with the soil that was taken from the first.

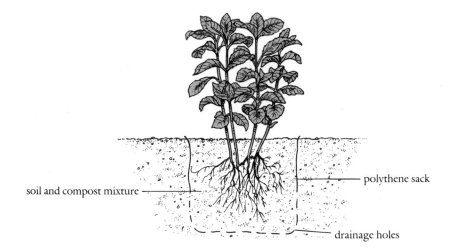

soil and compost mixture

polythene sack

drainage holes

Figure 11 Planting mint in a container to restrict its spread.

CHAPTER 6
PROPAGATING AND BUYING PLANTS

Propagating your own herbs, either from seed or from bits and pieces given to you by friends, can be great fun. Some get going very easily—you don't need to be a skilled horticulturalist! And it can be a cheap way to stock your garden, particularly for hedging and edging herbs where large numbers of plants of one kind are needed. This chapter describes methods of propagation you can try at home: a greenhouse is not necessary for just a few herbs, but for more it is certainly a big help.

You must, however, be prepared for some failures. It also takes longer to establish perennial plants if you grow them from scratch rather than buy plants. For single specimens it may be hardly economic to get a packet of seed, and better to visit your local nursery or order by post from one of the specialists as described on page 46.

As we have already seen, annual and biennial herbs must be raised from seed. Some perennials can also be obtained in this way although there may be problems: the seed may be tiny, slow to germinate or require certain special conditions such as very high temperatures, light or even a spell in your refrigerator. For some herbs, good germination is only achieved with very fresh seed, so you are at an immediate disadvantage when buying it in a packet from a shop.

Many perennials can be more easily propagated 'vegetatively': that is, from a parent plant by taking cuttings, layering or dividing it. New plants can be obtained more quickly in this way and they have the advantage of being identical to the parent plant, which is not necessarily the case with plants from seed. It is the only way to obtain some varieties of herbs whose characteristics are not seed-born, like variegated sages and thymes, or ones that do not produce seed at all, like lawn chamomile. Planting bulbs—of garlic or tree onion (Figure 12)—is also 'vegetative'

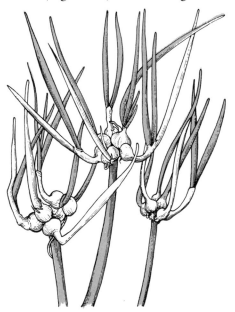

Figure 12 Tree onion showing the clusters of 'bulbils' which form on the tips of the leaves—these can be split up and planted.

propagation, and so is using the rhizomes (swollen underground stems) of the Florentine iris.

Sowing outdoors

Hardy annual and biennial herbs can be sown directly outside in the garden, and most are best treated in this way. They quickly become leggy if sown indoors in a pot and tend to bolt when transplanted. Some perennials also germinate easily outside: fennel, for example, will seed itself all over the herb garden. However, for just one or two plants it is generally easier to keep an eye on a pot in the greenhouse or on the windowsill. Annuals needed in quantity like parsley and dill (for dill seed) could be sown in a row in the vegetable garden; others, like chervil and rocket, need only a small patch in the herb garden.

Sowing

The first step is to produce a fine 'tilth' for sowing. If the bed has become compacted, fork it over first. Then use a rake to remove stones and break down the clods until the surface particles are the size of large breadcrumbs. This will be easy—even on a clay soil—if you pick a time when the soil is neither too wet and sticky nor baked dry. A small patch can always be protected from rain with a cloche, or watered if the weather is dry before sowing.

To sow a row, make a shallow drill with the corner of a hoe or rake along a taut string between two markers. A depth of between ¼–½ inch (6–13mm) is about right for most of the annual and biennial herbs: large seeds being buried deepest.

Sow the seeds *thinly*—two or three per inch is plenty—because germination tends to be an all or nothing affair: if conditions are right nearly all the seeds will germinate and will compete with one another for light and moisture; if conditions are wrong, none will germinate at all! After sowing, cover the drill gently with soil and lightly firm the surface with the back of the rake.

If creating a good tilth proves difficult, a practically foolproof way out is to line the bottom of a rough drill with peat or seed compost and cover the seeds with the same mixture. This is also useful on soils prone to 'capping', where the surface forms a hard crust after heavy rain.

For a patch of annuals in the herb garden, seed can be scattered over the soil surface and buried by raking gently in all directions. However, it is usually better to sow in a number of short closely spaced drills (as shown in Figure 13). This makes it easier to cover the seeds and to weed—especially if the seedlings are slow to emerge and you are not sure what they look like. The effect is the same once the plants have grown up. For tiny seeds like those of mullein or summer savory use moist peat in the drills and cover them only very thinly.

Germination

The conditions which seeds need for germination are moisture, air and warmth. A good tilth ensures that the seeds are in contact with the soil particles without being cemented in, thus satisfying the first two conditions. Remember the soil should be moist—but not waterlogged—before you start. Try *not* to water the seeds after they have been covered; if sowing in dry conditions is unavoidable, trickle water along the bottom of the drill before sowing and cover the seeds with dry soil. Small seeds sown near the soil surface can be covered with polythene to prevent them drying out; this must be removed as soon as the seedlings emerge.

Some seeds need more warmth to

Figure 13 Sowing a patch of annual herbs in the herb garden.

Break up compacted soil with a fork.

Rake it to a fine tilth.

Make a series of closely spaced drills with an onion hoe marking their positions with sticks.

Sow the seeds thinly, cover them with a fine layer of soil and lightly firm the surface with the back of the rake.

When the seedlings have emerged, thin them out and remove the sticks—it will look like an evenly sown area.

germinate than others and, in general, germination is quicker at higher temperatures. It is no use trying to sow dill or coriander, for example, in early spring when the soil is cold, whereas chervil and rocket will get going at much lower temperatures. Cloches or clear polythene put in position a week or two before sowing will help raise the soil temperature.

The main sowing months are March to May and again in August and September, this early autumn period being a good time to sow most of the biennials and herbs like chervil for winter use. Some perennials—particularly the native herbs like sweet cicely—are also best sown in the autumn, even though they do not emerge until the following spring. This is because the seeds need a period of cold before germination can occur. If autumn sowing is not practical you can give them a 'winter' in your refrigerator; mix them with damp sand and put them in a polythene bag or plastic container on the top shelf (*not* in the freezer) for six or eight weeks. Sowing times and conditions for individual herbs are given in Chapter 15.

Thinning

When the seedlings are large enough to handle, some should be removed gently so that the remainder stand well clear of one another; water them before doing this if the ground is dry. Later, when they are well established, thin to the final distance apart which will vary from herb to herb. Annual herbs grown as 'seedling crops' will not need thinning (see page 53).

Sowing indoors

By sowing seeds in pots in the house or greenhouse it is easier to give them the ideal conditions of warmth and mois-ture that they need.

Seed compost

It is essential to have a medium for sowing which retains moisture and does not pack down hard in the pot; it should also be as free as possible from weed seeds and disease spores. Garden soil is *not* suitable, nor is ordinary garden compost.

Nearly all the peat-based and soil-based (John Innes) composts sold in garden shops contain chemical fertilizers and are thus not organic. However, young seedlings do not need much feeding and an adequate sowing compost can be made by mixing two parts of moss peat with one part of coarse horticultural sand; sufficient nutrients will be provided by adding calcified seaweed or soaking the peat in a liquid seaweed solution diluted according to the manufacturer's recommendations for seedlings. If you do buy a proprietory compost, choose a soil-based one where at least some of the nutrients will be supplied naturally by the soil.

Sowing

For just one or two plants, seeds can be sown in small individual pots: either 2–3 inches (5–7.5cm) flower pots or plastic cartons thrown out from the kitchen (these must have drainage holes punched in the bottom). Fill them to the brim with loose moist compost, level it off and press the surface flat (Figure 14).

With seeds that can be handled—ones about the size of parsley—space three or four seeds over the area, then put a little compost through a coarse sieve to cover them lightly. For tiny seeds, scatter a small pinch over the surface and do not cover them. Stand the pots in a shallow tray of water until moisture seeps right up through the compost then allow them to drain.

Level off the compost and firm it using the bottom of another pot.

Space three or four seeds out over the surface and cover these lightly with coarsely sieved compost.

Stand the pots in a shallow tray of clean water until the surface becomes wet.

Figure 14 Sowing in individual pots of seed compost.

Germination

The pots must now be put somewhere warm and kept moist for the seeds to germinate. A temperature of around 60°F (15°C) is necessary for seeds of some of the half-hardy herbs and this temperature will also speed up the slow germinating herbs like parsley. Thus a heated propagator would be needed in a cold greenhouse in spring. Alternatively use a warm place indoors like a shelf near, but not directly on, a radiator. Cover the pots with polythene or glass to keep them moist.

An airing cupboard could also be used, because for most herbs darkness does not hinder germination and may even help it. (Pots in the light are often shielded with newspaper for this reason.) The pots must be checked every day and brought out as soon as any speck of white shoot shows. (Information on herbs which require light to germinate is limited, but celery and winter savory may be better left uncovered.)

Growing on

After the critical germination stage, the seedlings of many herbs can withstand much lower temperatures—the staging of a cold greenhouse for example—although half-hardy ones will need more warmth in spring. They *must* have good light, however, so if you are relying on your kitchen window sill, beware of sowing more plants than you have room for.

When the seedlings are growing well, nip off the surplus, leaving the strongest one in each pot to grow on. Keep the compost moist and feed them every few days with a liquid seaweed solution. If they start to look poorly or outgrow their pots before conditions are suitable to plant them out, transfer them to a larger pot using potting compost as described in Chapter 13.

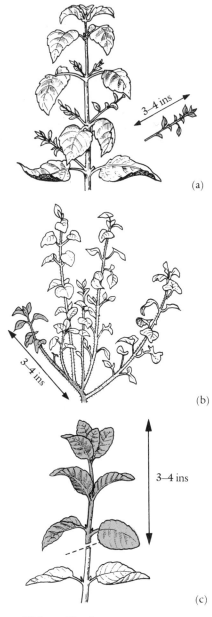

Figure 15 Stem Cuttings:
(a) a new side shoot of the required length;
(b) a new shoot from the crown of the plant;
(c) the tip of a long shoot cut just below a leaf joint.

If many plants of the same type are needed—perhaps for a herb hedge or edging—a large number of seeds can be germinated in the warmth in a 6-inch (15cm) pot or a seed tray, spacing them about ½ inch (13mm) apart. The seedlings should be 'pricked out' into individual pots as soon as they are large enough to handle, because they transplant with least check to growth at this stage.

Stem cuttings

Small shoots taken from some herbs will produce roots and grow if given the right conditions. This method is most suitable for the shrubby herbs like rosemary, sage and thyme; it will also work for some herbaceous herbs like mint, bergamot and lemon balm, although these are often better propagated in other ways. The best time to take cuttings is either in spring when strong new growth is being produced ('soft-shoot' cuttings), or in late summer after the herb has flowered when again there will be new shoots of herbaceous herbs and 'semi-ripe' shoots of shrubby herbs; ('semi-ripe' shoots are those that are beginning to harden at the base between the soft spring growth and harder older wood).

In all cases choose sturdy shoots with plenty of leaves: the length needed is about 3 to 4 inches (8–10cm). The ideal cutting is a side shoot of this length peeled off from the old stem, or one from the crown of a herbaceous plant (see Figures 15 and 16); the 'heel' of old growth helps stimulate new shoots. Alternatively for soft-shoot cuttings use the top few inches of longer shoots, severing them just below a leaf joint. (Avoid shoots that are too sappy or ones bearing flower buds as these seldom root well, even if the buds are removed.)

Sowing compost can be used for

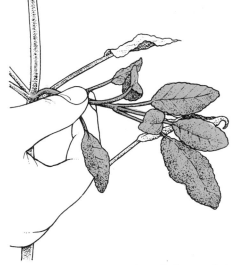

Figure 16 A 'semi-ripe' shoot being peeled off from the woody stem of a sage bush.

rooting cuttings (peat, sand and seaweed extract as described on page 40). No nutrients are needed, but the seaweed extract helps stimulate root growth. The hormone rooting powders sold in the shops contain synthetic plant hormones and also a fungicide, thus they are not something an organic gardener particularly wants to use; however, they may help with difficult cuttings.

Gently push the cuttings into the pots of moist compost as shown in Figure 17. Use a separate pot for each herb as some will take longer to root than others. Water them with a can and fine rose (it is essential to keep the atmosphere around them humid from now on) and put them in a warm place out of direct sunlight. A heated propagator in a greenhouse is ideal especially in spring. Indoors choose a shady window sill: stand the pots on a tray of coarse sand and spray them frequently with water or cover each loosely with a polythene bag to keep the atmosphere humid. A cold frame outdoors can be used for semi-ripe cuttings; it should be shaded and kept well watered in sunny weather.

Sappy cuttings, like those from mints, can root in two or three weeks in good conditions but expect those from, say, sage or rosemary to take a little longer. All of these root easily and you should expect a 90 per cent success rate. Semi-ripe cuttings can root in four to six weeks, but in a cold frame may need to be left until spring. Evergreens like bay may take up to twelve months and the success rate will probably be much lower.

When you see the first signs of new shoots or roots in one of the pots, bring it out in stages to normal sunny airy conditions. Tip out the contents, disturbing the roots as little as possible, and carefully separate the plants. They need some nutrients at this stage so mix an equal amount of good soil with the peat/sand sowing compost and pot them up individually: this should suffice until they have become established enough to plant out.

Layering

In this method of propagation, roots are encouraged to grow on the stems of shrubby herbs whilst they are still attached to the parent plant. It can be successful in cases where cuttings prove difficult to root.

Take a sturdy flexible branch close to the base of the plant, bend it over and roughen the stem at the point where it will touch the ground. Peg this point down and bury it, adding peat and sand if the soil is heavy (Figure 18a). When roots have formed, sever the branch joining the new plant from its parent; it can be potted up or moved straight to its new position, provided it is kept well watered.

An alternative method is 'mound layering'. This is very useful when

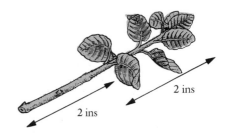

2 ins
2 ins

Peel the leaves from the bottom half of each cutting

Insert them to this depth round the edge of the pot of compost, spacing them about 2 inches (5cm) apart.

Cover the pot with a polythene bag, making sure this does not touch the cuttings; turn it inside out every few days when moisture builds up.

Figure 17 Rooting cuttings in a pot on a warm shady window sill.

(a) individual branches

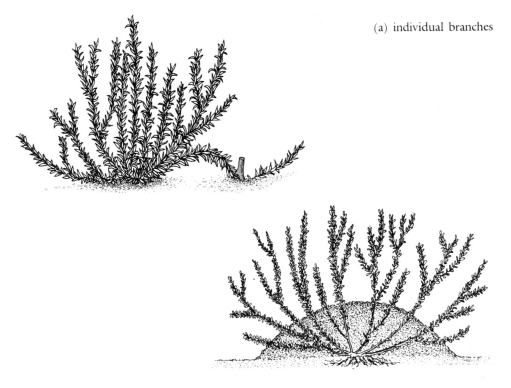

Figure 18 Layering.

dealing with old bushes of sage or thyme, for example, which have gone woody in the centre. In spring, heap earth (plus sand and peat if necessary) over the base of the plant until only the young shoots are showing (Figure 18b). By late summer roots should have formed on many of these shoots; they can be moved to new positions and the old plant dug up.

Division, offsets and root cuttings

Clumps of herbaceous herbs like lovage, lemon balm and mint can be divided in early spring or autumn when they are almost dormant. The ideal method is to lift the whole plant and gently ease it apart with two garden forks placed back to back. However, a spade can be used to slice pieces possessing both roots and shoots off a large clump while it is still in the ground; this may make the parent plant look shabby for a while. Clumps of herbs that grow from bulbs—like chives and tree onions—can also be divided in this way.

At the base of large clumps of comfrey, lovage and a few other herbaceous herbs, you will sometimes find small plantlets or 'offsets' which have both roots and shoots; these can be carefully pulled away and replanted.

All the mints can be propagated by division of the whole plant as described above. In fact, however, it is only necessary to have a small piece of root to reproduce a plant—as anyone who thought they had removed all traces of mint from a flower bed will know! A piece an inch or so in length (2.5cm) laid ½ inch (13mm) deep in a small pot of compost will soon produce shoots. Similar root cuttings can be taken of comfrey and horseradish.

Buying plants from nurseries

Most garden centres and nurseries stock a small range of common herbs. You will probably not find it difficult to buy lovage, angelica and lemon balm, for example, as well as the most familiar ones like parsley, sage, chives and thyme. Since most herbs survive well in pots, these are usually healthy and good value. Choose sturdy, bushy plants and inspect them for any signs of pests or disease (see Chapter 7). Also watch for mistaken labelling; at best, labels are likely to be uninformative with no Latin names given.

For other herbs it is best to visit a specialist herb nursery, of which there are now quite a few throughout the country. Some of these offer a mail order service. if you are buying in this way, look for accurate naming and descriptions in the catalogues. Beware, too, the 'substitutes' space on the order form: if you do not fill this in you may be sent unsuitable plants, particularly from small nurseries with lower stocks. Equally, however, they may have varieties not listed in the catalogue because supplies are limited. Either way it is worth a phone call to check on a special order. There is usually a high 'minimum order' price, so make a list from your herb garden plan and get all the herbs you need at one time.

When the plants arrive, unpack them straight away and check that the roots have not dried out. If there are any problems, write and inform the nursery immediately: most accept that there will be a certain loss in transit and allow for replacements. It may be best to cosset the herbs in pots for a few weeks before planting them out.

Hardening off and planting out

Plants that have been raised inside from seed or cuttings need to be acclimatized to outdoor conditions before planting out in spring or early summer. First put them out all day in a sheltered position and bring them in at night, finally leaving them out day and night just before planting. After this 'hardening-off' period, which should be about a week, the herb should transplant without much check to growth. Do not plant out half-hardy herbs until after the last frost. Established plants bought in pots can be planted out at any time during the growing season provided they are given sufficient attention.

Choose dull calm weather for planting if possible, or wait until the evening of a hot sunny day. The soil in the planting area should preferably be moist, so water in advance and let it drain if necessary. Also water the plant well. Make a hole just large enough to take the root ball and fill the soil in around it, gently firming it with your hands: it is important that no root damage occurs. Water a small area round the plant to wash soil into any air spaces left then make sure the plant is still firmly upright. Extra watering will be necessary for a few days in hot dry weather, particularly for lush herbs like mint and lemon balm.

CHAPTER 7
MAINTENANCE OF THE HERB GARDEN

An established organic herb garden does not take much time to look after as long as the site has been well prepared. Weeding will be mainly reduced to hoeing off annuals in spring before the plants bush out, and no regular feeding is necessary. The plants should be healthy so pests and diseases should not be a problem as long as you are on your guard (see pages 50-52).

A few herbs will need tying up, and most will need cutting back—but only once or twice during the growing season in an informal herb garden. Herb hedges and formal designs will require extra clipping. One main task in all types of garden is tidying up and preparing for winter.

Normal seasonal maintenance is made easier by keeping a long-term check on the plants and renewing them before they get too old or out of hand, as described on page 52.

Summer (June, July, August)
A new herb garden should be weeded rigorously while the plants are still small. Any perennial weeds left in when the site was cleared should be dug up carefully before they invade the roots of the herbs. Annual weeds round the larger plants should be hoed off or they will begin to compete for light and moisture. Patches of creeping herbs between paving will need regular hand weeding until the plants grow together to form a solid mat. In subsequent years

the amount of weeding necessary should become less and less.

In the first summer, watering may be necessary in a long dry period for the herbs to make good growth. Once they are established, however, many are very tolerant of drought: the aromatic herbs like rosemary, sage and thyme are naturally adapted to such conditions and ones with deep roots like lovage and fennel are equally able to cope. Among those which need watering in order to flourish are the mints, parsley, chives, bergamot, comfrey, angelica, sweet cicely and meadowsweet.

No fertilizers or liquid feeding should be needed provided the ground has been well prepared. Plants that look sickly or are recovering from a pest or disease attack can be given a 'tonic' of liquid seaweed: dilute this according to the manufacturer's directions for foliar feeding and water the plants using a watering can with a fine rose.

In the first year, little summer pruning will be necessary: clip the straggly ends of hedging herbs to encourage them to thicken up; trim the flower heads and any wayward branches from shrubby herbs when they have flowered. When picking herbs for use, always bear in mind the shape of the plant. Once the garden becomes established, however, much more cutting is necessary to keep the plants looking tidy and healthy (Figure 19).

Shrubby herbs—thymes, sage, savory,

(a) Cut round the outside of clumps of fennel, lovage, etc.;

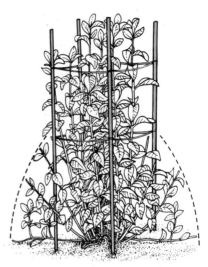

(b) Treat vigorous mints in a similar way—stake the tall centre—watch for creeping stems;

(c) Cut dead flower spikes from shrubby herbs. Trim new growth to shape and contain the bush.

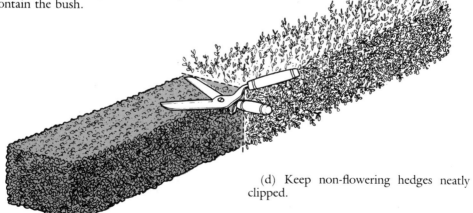

(d) Keep non-flowering hedges neatly clipped.

Figure 19 Summer pruning in the herb garden

lavender, hyssop—should be clipped round after they have flowered to remove the dead heads and maintain the shape of the bushes. If you have limited space, do not be afraid to keep the new growth cut right back: this will also help prevent herbs like sage and hyssop from developing bare woody centres. In a large informal garden, however, bushes can often be left to develop their characteristic shapes: the attractive grey-green spires of rosemary, for example.

Tall clumpy herbaceous herbs like lovage, tarragon, fennel and comfrey will almost certainly need cutting to restrict their growth. In a small garden, the whole plant can be cut back 1 to 2 feet (30–60cm) above the ground as fresh young shoots will soon grow up from the base. A better alternative is to cut round the outside of the clump, leaving the centre to grow up and flower: this looks tidy and attractive, and allows seeds to form and be collected. The tall centre may need to be staked in exposed positions. Treat vigorous mint plants in a similar way, and also watch for creeping, rooting overground stems: these should be cut off at the base of the plant and pulled away.

August and September are good months for sowing biennial and some perennial herbs (see page 38).

Autumn (September, October, November)
In early September, cut shrubby herbs and clip herb and box hedges for the last time—leave it later and the tender new growth subsequently produced could be damaged by frost.

Before the first frost, take in tender herbs like bay trees in pots, lemon verbena, and scented geraniums. Others may need some protection in late autumn before the weather gets too severe: young lemon thyme and rosemary bushes should be covered with cloches if possible; French tarragon is also susceptible if it is not well established, and can be protected by covering the crown with straw.

By this time the garden should have been finally cleared and weeded. Cut down the old growth and seed heads from perennial herbs which die down in winter: Umbellifers like lovage, fennel, sweet cicely and angelica; the mints, tarragon and chives. Completely clear the old annuals (like summer savory, borage, basil and dill) and the second year biennials (like parsley, mullein and caraway) which have gone to seed. Young parsley, chervil and rocket plants can be picked all through the winter if cloched and these, together with the few perennials, like salad burnet, which remain green are a valuable addition to winter salads.

October and early November are among the best times for lifting and dividing herbaceous herbs that have got too large (see page 45).

Winter (December, January, February)
Winter is a quiet time in the herb garden, but take advantage of this to do any construction work needed on paths, seats, steps or arches.

The empty spaces or beds used for sowing and planting annual herbs should be forked over: do this in early winter on heavy soils, but in February on light soils. Test the soil 'pH' every three or four years (as described on page 18) as the constant addition of compost, peat and leafmould will increase its acidity; lime should be aded in early winter if necessary. Herbaceous perennial herbs can be divided in February and March if they were not seen to in the autumn.

Spring (March, April, May)

In early spring the herb garden should be 'mulched'—that is, a layer of organic matter should be spread over the surface. Use well-rotted compost or manure on poor soils and round 'hungry' herbs like mint and chives; elsewhere use peat or leafmould. As well as feeding the plants, this mulch will help to improve the soil; it keeps the earthworms and micro-organisms active and retains the moisture. Provided it is itself free of weed seeds, the mulch will also suppress annual weeds.

From March onwards, sow the annual and biennial herbs that do not self-seed and put in any new or replacement plants. When all danger of frost has passed, plant out the half-hardy annuals like basil and bring out tender perennials like bay.

Cut out dead pieces from shrubby herbs. If any have become straggly and woody, now is the time to try cutting them back hard: rosemary, for example, should shoot even when cut back into the old wood, but you may have less success with sage: woody bushes of this herb are often better replaced (see page 52).

Pest and disease control

Herbs suffer from few pests and diseases—in fact many can be used in the vegetable garden to protect other crops. Plants that are grown in a well-cared for soil—one treated with compost and leaf mould rather than artificial fertilizers—are even less susceptible to attack. Most pests are kept in check by their natural enemies (like ladybirds and hoverflies which feed on aphids) as long as these are not destroyed by chemical sprays. Many useful insects find the herb garden attractive: hoverflies, for example, love to feed on the flowerheads of Umbellifers like fennel.

You can help tip this ecological balance further in your favour by general care of the herb garden. Always keep it well weeded, particularly in the autumn, as weeds can be both temporary hosts and overwintering homes for some pests. Similarly clear up all debris—this will particularly attract slugs. Try not to put plants under stress by sowing or planting them out at unsuitable times or in unsuitable positions, and keep them watered if necessary. For example, dryness will make some mints susceptible to powdery mildew, a white mould on the leaves and stems.

Be constantly on the look-out for pests, as the early stages of an attack can often be dealt with by 'physical' methods. Cabbage-white caterpillars on horseradish can simply be picked off by hand and destroyed; similarly the yellow and black caterpillars of the mullein moth, which will otherwise soon reduce a handsome grey mullein plant to sad tatters (Figure 20a). Leaf miners are sometimes a problem on lovage, wild celery and sorrel: these grubs eat winding tunnels in the leaves which are clearly visible (Figure 20b). Watch for the first tunnels, pick off the affected leaves and destroy them, otherwise the tunnels will extend to broad dry patches and complete leaves will wither away.

Scale insects are often noticeable as immobile waxy brown humps gathered near the leaf veins or on the stems of bay trees; the leaves also become covered with a sticky, sooty mould. Rub the scales off gently before the infestation builds up.

Yellowing or wilting leaves and stunted growth of any Umbellifers may be a sign of attack by the grubs of the carrot fly, which will tunnel into the roots. Parsley in the vegetable garden may be particularly vulnerable, and here plants should be pulled up and destroyed to get rid of the pest. Large herbs in the herb garden should over-

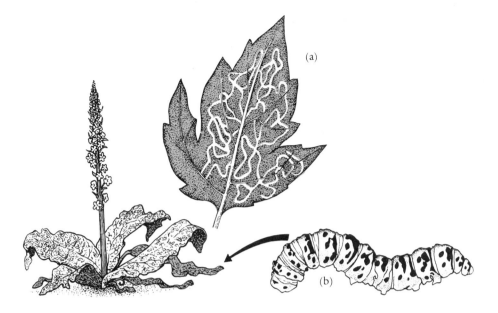

Figure 20 Pests in the herb garden: (a) leaf miner tunnels in a lovage leaf; (b) damage from mullein moth caterpillar.

come attacks: pick off dead leaves and feed the plant with liquid seaweed solution.

Slugs are not attracted to many of the coarse dry aromatic herbs, but can be a problem with lush young plants. Slug numbers can be reduced by trapping them in a sunken saucer of a sweet liquid—beer is best but milk or sugar and water will do! Small transplants can be protected for a couple of weeks by covering them with makeshift open-topped cloches cut from plastic lemonade bottles. However, a certain amount of tolerance is part of the organic approach to pest and disease control: it is better, for example, to put up with a few holes in the large lower leaves of a sorrel plant than to use a chemical slug killer.

Diseases can also sometimes be dealt with by physical methods. One of the commonest found in the herb garden is mint rust—a fungus which causes orange patches of spores on the leaves. These drop onto the soil surface and will infect new shoots the following spring. They can, however, be destroyed by packing dry straw amongst the dying mint stalks in the autumn and setting light to it. Comfrey suffers from a similar rust disease and here the best answer is to keep the plant clipped (cutting off the leaves every four weeks) and well fed with manure and compost.

If, despite all preventative measures, a pest or disease attack begins to get out of hand, there are 'organic' insecticides and fungicides that can safely be used. These are of vegetable origin and thus do not contaminate the herbs or their environment; properly used, they will also spare most of the predators, parasites and bees which are the gardener's friends.

Derris is the main standby. It is easily available as a liquid or a dust and is an effective killer of aphids like greenfly, whitefly and blackfly, of young scale insects and of small caterpillars. It is harmless to bees and to hoverfly larvae, and to human beings too. A dilution of soap flakes or even washing up liquid can also be surprisingly effective against aphids.

The best caterpillar killer is a 'biological' spray which contains the spores of a bacteria *Bacillus thuringiensis*: this is deadly to most caterpillars but completely safe for all other life in the garden. It is sold as a powder which is made up and used just like a chemical spray.

Slug killers are more of a problem, but there is one based on aluminium silicate which—although not strictly organic—is preferable to the usual slug pellets. The small white crystals should be dissolved in water and sprayed round the plants with a watering can.

There are no organic fungicides that can be bought in the shops, but a brew of elder leaves is an old remedy worth trying against mildew (see page 92).

Replacing perennial herbs

Long-term maintenance of the herb garden must allow for the fact that some perennials are relatively short-lived. The life span of angelica, for example, is generally from two to five years, and it is thus wise to plant another—or let a self-sown seedling grow up—in its second winter.

Regular clipping as described on pages 47-49 helps keep shrubby herbs looking young and healthy but some—like sage—still tend to become woody in the centre. They are best replaced by new plants every four or five years. As well as being more attractive, young plants are often less susceptible to damage in winter. You should be able to grow most of them yourself from cuttings as described on pages 43-46.

The herbaceous herbs, like fennel, lovage and tarragon, need lifting and dividing every four or five years to prevent them becoming too large; sometimes old clumps also seem to lose their flavour. Discard the old centre and replant with several young pieces from the edge of the clump, in a different position if possible. Rich feeding plants, especially the mints, tend to exhaust the soil, so take the opportunity to work in some well-rotted compost before replanting where these have been.

CHAPTER 8
HARVESTING AND PRESERVING

The summer abundance of fresh herbs is delightful but deceiving: most of them die down all too soon, and only a very few can be picked during the winter. It is thus well worth preserving some from your own garden—either by drying or freezing, or by capturing their flavour in oils, vinegar and syrups. The results can be far superior to shop-bought products and the scope is much greater: you can use a wide variety of herbs and also different parts of the plant—not only leaves, but seeds, flowers, stalks and roots (Table 8). The herbs are also free from harmful traces of pesticides and fungicides.

The techniques of harvesting and preserving herbs are aimed towards retaining as many of the original constituents as possible: culinary herbs must keep their colour and flavour, *pot-pourri* herbs their scent, and medicinal herbs their healing powers. Thus the herbs must be carefully handled at all stages.

Harvesting
Leaves
When picking leaves for immediate use, always consider the shape of the plant. Pinch out the tips of bushy herbs like basil to encourage the plants to thicken out; pick the outside leaves and stalks from herbs which grow only from the base, like parsley and lovage, leaving fresh young shoots to grow out from the centre crown. Some annual herbs can be grown in relatively thick patches and the very young leaves cut when they are only about 1 to 3 inches (2.5–7.5cm) high. Such 'seedling crops' are tender with a good flavour, and many will resprout at least once after cutting. Examples are coriander, dill and rocket.

Larger quantities of leaves can be taken from established plants for drying and freezing: annuals and herbaceous perennials can be cut right across: say to about 1 foot (30cm) above the ground for clumps of fennel and lovage, and to about 4 inches (10cm) for basil and summer savory. The new growth of shrubby herbs can be cut back by about a third shaping the bushes at the same time.

Ideally, the harvest should take place when the leaves are in peak condition and, for aromatic herbs, contain the maximum amount of volatile oil. The exact time when this occurs varies from plant to plant, but is generally just before flowering. However, harvesting at any time when the herbs are growing strongly will give satisfactory results: obviously it is not good to weaken the plant in early spring, and tatty autumn leaves will have lost all their powers. The last cut of evergreen perennial herbs should not be taken later than early September so that any subsequent growth made by the plant has time to 'harden' before the first frost. Although sprigs can be picked occasionally during the winter, their flavour will generally

Table 8: The herb harvest: parts of the plants other than the leaves which are commonly used

Stems	Flowers	Fruits	Seeds	Roots
Angelica	Bergamot	Elderberries	Caraway	Angelica
Fennel	Borage	Juniper berries	Celery	Chicory
Sweet cicely	Chamomile	Nasturtium	Coriander	Comfrey
	Elderflower	(green seed pods)	Dill	Dandelion
	Hops	Rosehips	Fennel	Elecampane
	Lavender		Lovage	Horseradish
	Marigold		Mustard	
	Meadowsweet			
	Mullein			
	Nasturtium			
	Rose			

be poor.

The time of day also affects the amount of aromatic oil in the leaves: it is at its peak on a dry morning, before heat and sunshine have taken their toll. Wait until any early dew has gone then cut the foliage cleanly, put it carefully into a shallow basket or on to a tray and carry it indoors immediately out of the sun.

Washing should be avoided where possible. If the foliage is dusty or splashed with soil, it may be possible to spray it clean on the plant and leave it to dry naturally before harvest. Otherwise, rinse out leaves quickly in cold water and spread them out on tea towels to dry thoroughly.

Flowers

The flowers of herbs like thyme, rosemary, savory and mint are sometimes gathered, dried and used along with the foliage. When herb flowers have a separate use, however, the time for harvest is fairly critical. Marigold, borage, bergamot and elderflowers should be picked when they are well out but before they are mature. Lavender spikes should be cut when about half the flowers are open. As with leaves, handle them carefully as they are easily bruised.

Stems

The herb stems that are most commonly used are angelica (for candying—to make the familar green cake decoration) and fennel (generally dried for use in baking). Stems of angelica are ready in early summer as soon as they have thickened. Fennel stems can be cut from midsummer onwards—even the dry autumn stalks will be of some use for barbecues.

Seeds

The seeds of herbs like dill and coriander are concentrated sources of flavour and are much easier to store than leaves. However, the strength of some herb seeds means that they must be treated with caution: for example, parsley seeds contain dangerous amounts of the volatile oil 'apiol'. Seeds of annuals and some perennials can also be saved for resowing: this is particularly useful where a large amount of seed (for broadcasting) or very fresh seed is needed.

In dry weather, wait as long as possible before harvesting and then snip off the whole seed-head just before the seeds begin to fall: it is particularly important to have ripe seeds for propagation, but even culinary seeds will have more flavour and keep better when

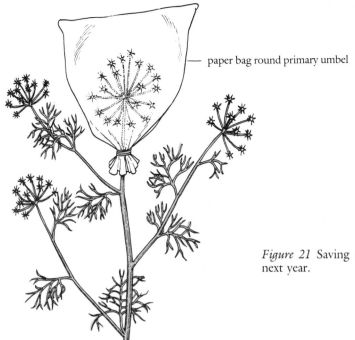

— paper bag round primary umbel

Figure 21 Saving dill seed for sowing the next year.

Figure 22 Storing seed for resowing.

silica gel crystals

DILL
1985

truly ripe. Seeds for resowing should also be chosen from the strongest, healthiest plants; keep these well watered whilst the seeds are forming. For Umbellifers, seeds from the top 'primary' umbel may give better germination in some cases. Stake the plant and put a paper bag over the whole seed-head if the weather is dry but wind threatens to beat you to the harvest (Figure 21).

Roots

Herb roots, like those of horseradish, are usually dug in the autumn when they are fattest—full of food stored for the winter—but they *can* be lifted at any time. Obviously all or part of the plant is destroyed when roots are harvested, so keep some pieces for replanting. Wash the rest carefully.

Drying

Leaves, flowers and stems

Slow drying is the traditional way to preserve the foliage and flowers of herbs. Those with small dry leaves—like thyme and savory—keep their flavour best but some others give good results (see Table 9). Flowers like marigold, elder and bergamot also dry well.

Success depends on drying off the moisture as quickly as possible without damaging the plant tissues—thus soft tender herbs like basil are more difficult to dry well. Not only warmth, but a good circulation of air, darkness and a clean atmosphere are necessities. The temperature should ideally be between 70° and 90°F (21°–33°C).

It remains to find somewhere in the home which will provide these conditions. Obviously a sunny greenhouse or a steamy kitchen are not the places to choose. In summer, an attic or a dark outbuilding like a tool-shed may be suitable. Hang herb foliage in small bunches from a line or spread it out on slatted wooden trays lined with newspaper or thin cotton. Flowers should be laid out in a single layer on similar drying trays. The danger is that in bad weather they will take too long to dry and become musty and dusty. Some artificial heat is then necessary: use an electric greenhouse fan heater or a similar source of background heat in the outbuilding if a power supply is available (do not use a paraffin or calor gas heater as these create dampness and a smell that could taint the herbs). Small quantities of herbs can be dried in an airing cupboard if the door is left ajar for ventilation; alternatively try the plate-warming drawer of an oven, again with the door slightly open. If any of the leaves go brown, then the temperature is too high: check it with a thermometer if possible.

The time needed for drying depends on the herb and the temperature. In good conditions delicate herbs like basil should be dry in about three days—any longer and the flavour will probably suffer. Thicker leaves like those of sage and tough stems can take one or two weeks and the results will still be satisfactory. Leaves and stems are ready for storing when they become brittle, and flowers when they rustle to the touch. Do not be disheartened by initial failures: there is an art to drying herbs, but it is easily mastered·just by experimenting with different herbs in different drying conditions.

One other far from traditional way of drying herbs is by using a microwave oven. The results can be surprisingly good—herbs such as parsley and tarragon which are difficult to dry by conventional methods keep their colour and flavour well. Obtaining a green, pungent basil, however, is still difficult and it is debatable whether the results for the coarser aromatic herbs are any better than those from slow drying under good conditions. However, the

Table 9: Methods for preserving the foliage of culinary herbs: these choices should give a good useful product in each case but are not necessarily exclusive.

Drying	Freezing	Oils	Vinegars	Syrups	Picked all year round
Bay	Chervil	Basil	Dill	Peppermint	Chervil (if cloched)
Bergamot	Chives	Fennel	Mint		Lamb's lettuce
Lemon verbena	Dill	Rosemary	Nasturtium		Parsley (if cloched)
Lemon balm	Fennel	Thymes	Salad burnet		Rosemary (from large bushes)
Lovage	Parsley		Tarragon		Sage (from large bushes)
Mints	Sorrel		Thymes		Salad burnet
Rosemary	Tarragons				
Sage					
Savories					
Sweet marjoram					
Thymes					

process is quick and easy—most herbs take about three minutes to dry, depending on how thick the leaves are and how much they are spread out. Again it is best to experiment: set the oven for two minutes initially, then check to see how brittle the leaves have become; if necessary repeat for further intervals of one minute until they are ready.

Seeds

Seed-heads should be dried naturally in a warm airy place; they do not need to be in the dark. Lay them on drying trays or hang them up, putting newspaper below to catch loose seeds. When they are thoroughly dry—usually after two or three weeks—rub them from their stalks or separate them by threshing.

Roots

Roots need some artificial heat for drying, and temperatures slightly higher than those recommended for leaves can be used. Thin roots should be cut into small pieces and thick ones finely sliced. They are ready for storing when they are brittle right through.

Storing dried herbs

The best storage containers are dark glass jars and glazed pots with tight lids, as these exclude both air and light:

bright light causes the colour and flavour of dried herbs to deteriorate. Plastic and tin containers are sometimes said to taint the herbs but in practice this is rarely a problem, although these containers look less attractive on the kitchen shelf. Clear glass jars should only be used if they are kept in a dark cupboard—a fact that many manufacturers of herbal products seem to ignore.

Herb leaves can be stripped from tough or woody stems for storing, but do not crumble them more than necessary as this releases valuable volatile oils. It is useful to keep whole sprigs of herbs like thyme for tying into *bouquet garni* (see page 63), and the stalks of herbs such as bergamot that are to be used for making teas need not be discarded: they may need further drying but can then be cut into short lengths and stored. Label all containers so you can identify them quickly (by eye rather than by smell!), and date them too, because all stocks should be replaced by freshly dried supplies the next summer. Seeds and roots for household use can be similarly stored in pots or glass jars.

Seeds for resowing need to be kept as dry and cold as possible otherwise they will lose their 'viability' (their ability to germinate). Put them in labelled and dated envelopes and keep them in an airtight jar or box in which you have put a small open container of silica gel (Figure 22). The silica gel crystals, which can be bought from most chemists shops, take up moisture from the air in the jar, hence drying it. (Crystals which have been treated with cobalt chloride turn from blue to pink when moist; they can then be dried in an oven for two or three hours and returned to the jar.) Keep the jar in a cool place. Many herb seeds will keep for two or three years if stored like this, although there are exceptions: angelica, for example, needs to be sown as soon after harvest as possible.

Freezing

Freezing is a quick and easy method of preserving which works well for the leaves of most culinary herbs. Even those that are difficult to dry—like parsley, chives, and tarragon—keep their colour and flavour well, and if freezer space is short, it is best reserved for these herbs.

It is not necessary to blanch them: simply pop whole sprigs into polythene bags and straight into the freezer; they can be crumbled up for use while still frozen. Either keep each type separate and carefully labelled, or put together the mixtures you use most: perhaps chervil, parsley and tarragon for omelettes, and thyme, parsley and marjoram for stews.

An alternative method is to chop the herbs and freeze them into ice-cubes (use a liquidizer to prepare large quantities). They are then ready to stir straight into soups and stews. Herbs like mint and salad burnet can be frozen into novelty ice-cubes for fruit drinks. The cubes can be stored in polythene bags in the freezer. Some flowers for medicinal use like elderflower and mullein can also be successfully frozen.

Oils, vinegars and syrups

Oils and vinegars are an excellent way of capturing the flavour of culinary herbs, and are quick and easy to add to a whole variety of cooked dishes and salads. Oils and alcohol are similarly used to extract the active substances in some medicinal and cosmetic herbs.

Either individual herbs, combinations of herbs, or mixtures of herbs and spices can be used. Exact quantities and methods can vary from herb to herb and according to convenience: some examples are given in Chapters 9 and 11 and Table 10. The following is a general guide on which to base your own experiments.

Oils

A wide-necked jar is packed with lightly bruised herb leaves and filled up with a suitable vegetable oil. For medical and cosmetic preparations, almond oil is an excellent base or, alternatively, use a light sunflower oil. For these preparations the jar should be put in a warm sunny place for one to two weeks. Shake or stir the contents daily. At the end of this time the vegetable oil will have absorbed most of the aromatic herbal oil and can be strained off. For more strength, repeat the process with fresh herbs.

It is often recommended that oils for culinary use are also made in this way. However, the exposure to light and warmth causes the deterioration of the oil, especially with the unsaturated oils like sunflower and sesame oil that are best for herbal extractions because of their mild flavour. It is therefore preferable to leave the herb to infuse slowly in a cool dark place, even though this sacrifices some of the flavour.

Culinary herb oils can be used in salad dressings, for roasting meats, in bread and savoury biscuits—in fact to add flavour to any dishes where veget-

Table 10: Methods for preserving medicinal and cosmetic herbs—flowers (F), leaves (L), and roots (R)

Drying	Freezing	Oils	Alcoholic preparations	Syrups	Harvested all year round
Elder (F)	Elder (F)	Rosemary (L)	Elder (F)	Elder (F)	Horseradish (R)
Chamomile (F)	Mullein (F)	Marigold (F)	Horseradish (R)	Peppermint (L)	Sage (L)
Meadowsweet (L,F)	Comfrey (L)				Rosemary (L)
Comfrey (L)					
Lady's mantle (L)					
Peppermint (L)					
Rosemary (L)					
Sage (L)					
Hops (F)					
Raspberry (L)					
Yarrow (F,L)					

able oils would normally be used. Medicinal and cosmetic oils are used externally as rubbing oils for aches and pains, or as skin conditioners.

Vinegars and extracts in alcohol

Whereas oils will carry quite delicate flavours, vinegars are best used to preserve herbs that have a distinctive taste or that compliment the sharpness of the vinegar. Use a fine wine vinegar as a base if possible, or otherwise cider vinegar.

The basic method is the same as for oils: the herb leaves are left to steep for about two weeks while the vinegar absorbs the flavour. (Some recipes recommend using hot vinegar or simmering the herb with the vinegar.) It is then strained off through muslin or a filter paper to get a really clear liquid, and bottled. A fresh sprig of the herb is added to each bottle for decoration and identification. Herb vinegars are useful mainly for marinades and salad dressings, although flower vinegars—like elderflower—are sometimes suggested for flavouring sweet dishes.

Some herbal remedies can be conveniently prepared in the form of alcoholic extracts of the fresh herbs. For example, a good preparation for elderflowers is to steep them in five times their weight of white wine for two weeks; vodka or white rum (with a higher alcohol content) makes a suitable base for an extract of horseradish root using the same proportions.

Syrups

Vinegar and alcohol are thus used to preserve the active ingredients of the herbs from decay—just like in vegetable pickles. The other familiar way of preserving is to use sugar—as in fruit jams—and this too can be used for herbs.

Herb syrups are easily made by dissolving sugar in a herbal infusion. Pack the herb leaves or flowers loosely into a measuring jug and pour on boiling water. Leave it covered to infuse for five or ten minutes and then strain. Add sugar, using about 1 lb (455g) to 1 pint (570ml) of liquid and dissolve it by warming. Pour the syrup into bottles, cleaned thoroughly with boiling water, and seal them immediately.

The syrups are mainly used medicinally, making a remedy that is soothing and pleasant to take. Some (like elderflower) can be diluted for drinks or used to flavour sweet dishes.

CHAPTER 9
THE CULINARY HERB GARDEN

Herbs can transform almost any ordinary dish into something special: not just main course roasts and stews, but soups and sweets, vegetables and salads, bread and biscuits. Fresh from the garden, they easily become a natural ingredient of every meal from the quick snack to the dinner party: chopped as a simple garnish to plain or 'convenience' foods or cooked with an elaborate dish to impart flavour.

Some herbs are strong and should be treated with caution at first; others can be used with abandon. But there are no strict rules. Traditional associations like sage with onion are only the start. Experimenting with different combinations and quantities is all part of the fun of herb cookery: the recipes in this chapter are just to whet your appetite!

Garden design

A possible design for a small culinary herb garden is shown in Figure 23a. This design could be useful for borders outside the kitchen door or on a small terrace near the house. Even this small area can provide enough of the frequently used culinary herbs for day-to-day use. The larger herbs would have to be clipped regularly to keep them in check: plants for seed, drying and freezing, and extra salad herbs could be grown in the vegetable garden. The beds in this small garden could be made into raised beds. A garden which has been newly planted to a similar design is shown in Figure 23b. This garden is surrounded by low brick walls to provide shelter.

Figure 24 shows a design for a complete culinary herb garden consisting of a number of narrow beds. All the herbs can be reached from the gravel path. The herbs are roughly divided into strong aromatic culinary herbs, mild cooking herbs, sweet herbs, and salad herbs. A herb hedge of closely clipped winter savory (or a purely decorative box) unites the beds.

In both designs sun-loving herbs are put on the south side of tall herbs, and those that can tolerate partial shade are placed behind them.

Equipment for herb cookery

Herbs need little skilled preparation. The most important utensils are a sharp knife, scissors, and a chopper: the special semi-circular choppers that fit into wooden bowls will do small quantities quickly and cleanly (Figure 25). A liquidizer is useful for chopping large quantities to go into soups or stews (simply blend them with a little of the cooking liquid or water). A pestle and mortar are the traditional implements for pounding herbs and grinding seeds, although the end of a rolling pin will often suffice. A garlic crusher, however, is well worth buying: it is quick and easy to use, and there is no fear of garlic tainting other utensils.

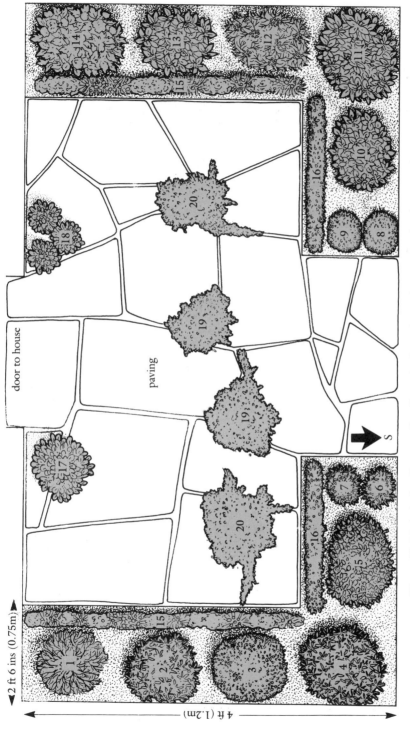

Figure 23 (a) A design for a small culinary herb garden, using narrow borders round a terrace adjacent to the house.

Key: 1 fennel; 2 French tarragon; 3 chervil; 4 rosemary; 5 sweet marjoram; 6 winter savory; 7 summer savory; 8 garden thyme; 9 lemon thyme; 10 pot marjoram; 11 sage; 12 dill; 13 spearmint; 14 lovage; 15 edging of parsley and chives; 16 edging of salad burnet; 17 bay tree; 18 pots of basil; 19 creeping lemon thyme; 20 creeping caraway thyme.

Figure 23 (b) An example of a garden planted to a design similar to *Figure 23* (a).

Quantities and qualities

The quantities of herbs required for recipes can only be a rough guide: the strength and flavour of fresh herbs varies with the season and how they are grown, and the quality of dried herbs is even more variable. The amounts needed also depend very much on personal taste. It is the cook who, with experience, can make the best decision!

The herb flavour should never dominate but should help bring out the true flavour of the dish. The best guide is first to identify the few particularly pungent herbs, like sweet marjoram and basil, which should be used sparingly until their flavour is familiar (Table 11). These herbs do not combine well with each other—use only one per dish. More moderate herbs like rosemary and lovage should similarly be treated with caution at first, although some recipes do call for relatively large quantities.

Other herbs can be used lavishly: in salads, for garnishing or in cooked dishes. They can be used in combination with each other and with the stronger herbs. Parsley and chervil, for example, enhance the flavour of any herb with which they are mixed. Good examples are the ubiquitous *'bouquet garni'* for stews (a mixture of thyme, parsley, bay and marjoram, traditionally as sprigs tied together with string) and the *'fine herbes'* mixture for omelettes (chopped parsley, chervil, tarragon and chives); use more parsley and chervil, and less of the stronger herbs in both cases. Angelica and sweet cicely leaves can be stewed in relatively large amounts with fruit, the idea being to offset the tartness of the fruit rather than to impart flavour.

The association of particular herbs and foods—the sage and onion stuffing mentioned earlier—extends to less familiar herbs too, and is a good way to start using these stranger flavours. Try basil in tomato sauce for a pizza with a real Italian flavour, or chop it raw with tomato salad. Savory is the herb for beans: add a sprig of fresh savory to runner beans as they cook; use dried savory in a winter hot-pot of haricots or even with tinned baked beans! These are not the only ways of using the herbs of course but they provide a useful base for your own experiments.

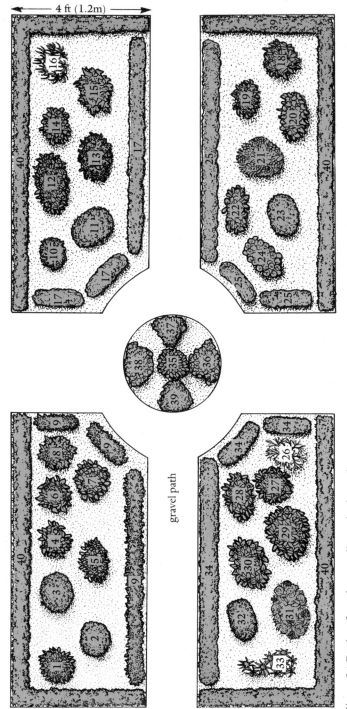

Figure 24 Design for a large culinary herb garden

Key—*Sweet herbs:* 1 rosemary; 2 lemon thyme; 3 sweet cicely; 4 peppermint; 5 heartsease pansies; 6 borage; 7 lemon balm; 8 angelica; 9 alpine strawberries edging.

Mild cooking herbs: 10 pot marjoram; 11 chervil; 12 spearmint; 13 French tarragon; 14 apple mint; 15 good king Henry; 16 tree onion; 17 salad burnet and parsley mixed edging.

Mild salad herbs: (18 horseradish); 19 rocket; 20 sorrel; 21 dill; 22 lamb's lettuce; 23 purslane; 24 nasturtium; 25 salad burnet and parsley mixed edging.

Strong aromatic herbs: 26 fennel; 27 Russian tarragon; 28 sage; 29 lovage; 30 basil; 31 caraway; 32 coriander; 33 garlic; 34 thyme and sweet marjoram mixed edging.

Centre piece: 35 bay tree; 36 lemon scented geranium; 37 caraway creeping thyme; 38 rose-scented geranium; 39 lemon creeping thyme.

Hedge: 40 winter savory.

A herb garden in a sheltered corner by the house with access from stone paths; the hedge is of lavender 'Munstead Dwarf'.

Some medicinal herbs cut for drying: (from left to right) meadowsweet, red sage, yarrow (below), lady's mantle (above), peppermint (below), raspberry leaves (above); dried herbs should be stored in dark glass or pottery jars.

Preserving the flavour of herbs in oils and vinegars: (from left to right) dill-pickled cucumbers, basil and garlic oil, tarragon vinegar.

A sundial is the centrepiece of this herb garden which has beds surrounded by closely clipped box hedges and walls covered in climbing roses.

A circular layout round a fountain and small pond.

Table 11: A guide to the strength of culinary herbs (these are not rigid categories!)

Pungent aromatic herbs	*Moderate aromatic herbs*	*Mild garnishing and salad herbs*	*Mild cooking herbs*
Basil	Dill	Chervil	Angelica
Bay	Fennel	Chives	Good King Henry
Caraway	Lovage	Lamb's lettuce	Mint
Coriander	Rosemary	Nasturtium	Pot marjoram
Garlic	Savory	Parsley	Sweet cicely
Sage	Tarragon	Purslane	Tree onion
Sweet marjoram		Rocket	
Thyme		Salad burnet	
		Sorrel	

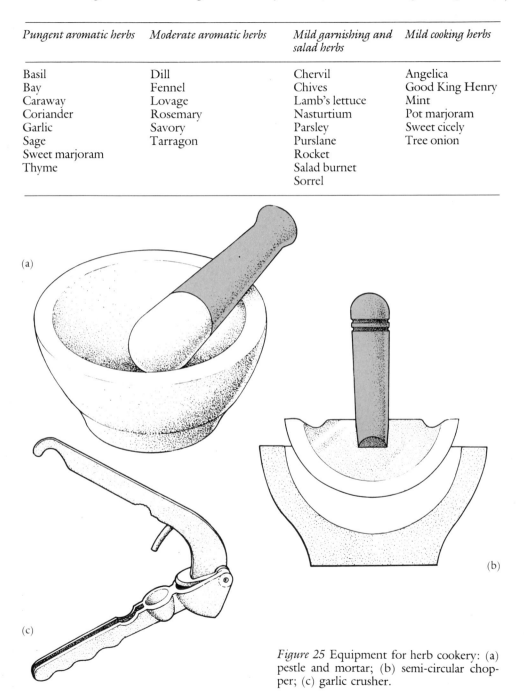

(a)

(b)

(c)

Figure 25 Equipment for herb cookery: (a) pestle and mortar; (b) semi-circular chopper; (c) garlic crusher.

HERB RECIPES

SOUPS

Herbs are ideal for use in soups, immediately counteracting any blandness. The stronger herbs—fresh or dried—are usually prepared and cooked with the other ingredients: liquidized for a creamy soup or strained out of a clear one. The more delicate herbs, freshly chopped or frozen, should be added uncooked just before serving to provide an appetizing contrast of colour as well as flavour: try lovage, chervil or salad burnet as alternatives to the more commonly used parsley and chives. Single herbs rather than mixtures tend to be the most effective. Occasionally the herb itself is a major ingredient—sorrel soup being the traditional (French) example.

CELERY AND LOVAGE SOUP

1 onion, chopped
2 sticks celery, chopped
6 fresh lovage leaves or
  1 tablespoon dried
½ pint (285ml) vegetable stock or water
½ oz (15g) butter
½ oz (15g) wholemeal flour
½ pint (285ml) milk
Fresh lovage, chopped, to garnish

1. Cook chopped onion, celery and lovage in the vegetable stock until soft. Liquidize.
2. Melt the butter in a pan. Add the flour to make a roux and cook for a few minutes.
3. Gradually add the milk, stirring all the time. Then add the liquidized vegetables.
4. Reheat and serve, garnished with fresh chopped lovage.

SORREL SOUP

2 oz (55g) butter
4 oz (115g) sorrel, chopped
4 oz (115g) spinach or lettuce, chopped
2 oz (55g) parsley, chopped
4 oz (115g) potato, peeled and thinly sliced
1 pint (570ml) vegetable stock
Sea salt and freshly ground black pepper
4 tablespoons single cream

1. Melt the butter in a pan, add the chopped sorrel, spinach (or lettuce) and parsley and cook for a few minutes.
2. Add the sliced potato and vegetable stock. Simmer until the potato slices are soft and then liquidize.
3. Reheat, season to taste and add the cream before serving.

SALADS

A salad with fresh herbs is not only delicious but an important part of a healthy diet. In summer, the mild herbs can add endless variations to the basic home-grown salad ingredients (Table 11). Several herbs can be picked in winter to give welcome greenness to salads of grated roots and white cabbage; many others begin shooting in early spring, long before the first garden lettuce. Dried herbs are sometimes suitable salad ingredients: marjoram is commonly sprinkled over Greek salads made of soft cheese on a base of fleshy tomatoes and white cabbage or cucumber. Herb oils and vinegars are particularly useful for salad dressings when fresh herbs are not available.

WINTER HERB SALAD

White cabbage or celeriac
Chervil
Parsley
Sunflower or sesame seeds
Sunflower oil
Lemon juice
Salad burnet leaves, stripped from stalks

1. Shred the white cabbage or, alternatively, grate the celeriac.
2. Chop the chervil and parsley. Toast the sunflower or sesame seeds.
3. Mix the sunflower oil and lemon juice to make a dressing.
4. Place the cabbage, herbs and seeds in a bowl and toss in the oil and lemon dressing.

POTATO AND SORREL SALAD

Sorrel
Chives
Eggs, hard-boiled
New potatoes, cooked and cooled
Natural yogurt or mayonnaise, or both
Nasturtium leaves and flowers

1. Shred the sorrel and chop the chives and hard-boiled eggs. Mix together with the cooled potaoes and lightly fold in the dressing.
2. Pile onto an attractive serving dish and garnish around the edge with nasturtium leaves and flowers.

EGGS AND CHEESE

Delicate herbs like tarragon and chervil can be well appreciated in otherwise indistinctive egg dishes. The obvious example is omelette with *fines herbes* (page 63). Curd and cottage cheese are often mixed with fresh chopped herbs: usually chives, but lovage or dill gives an interesting unusual flavour. The pungent herbs, sage in particular, are more suitable for cooked dishes using strong hard cheeses.

COURGETTE BAKE

1 lb (455g) courgettes, thinly sliced
4 eggs
4 oz (115g) grated cheese
Sea salt and freshly ground black pepper
Chervil, chives and pot marjoram,
    freshly chopped

1. Steam the courgettes lightly for about 5 minutes. Then place in a greased baking dish.
2. Beat the eggs, then mix in the grated cheese, seasoning and herbs.
3. Pour over the steamed courgettes and bake at 325°F/170°C (Gas Mark 3) until set (about 30 minutes).

STUFFED EGGS

Hard-boiled eggs, 1 for each person
Curd or cottage cheese
A little cream or butter
Dill leaves, finely chopped
Sea salt and freshly ground black pepper
Cucumber slices

1. Cut the eggs lengthways and remove the yolks. Place these in a bowl with an equal quantity of curd or cottage cheese and beat together, adding a little cream or butter if necessary to give a soft consistency.
2. Stir in the chopped dill leaves—use a very small amount at first and add more if the flavour is not too strong. Season to taste.
3. Pile the mixture back into the egg halves and serve on a bed of cucumber slices.

VEGETABLES

The simple use of a few herbs helps make vegetables an important part of a meal, rather than a mere accompaniment. Use the delicate herbs individually, freshly chopped and added to vegetables before serving. Try salad burnet with carrots, chervil with cauliflower, and dill with beetroot.

Stronger herbs (dried or fresh) are usually added during cooking: a sprig of savory with beans, thyme with cabbage, or basil with tomatoes. Frozen vegetables also benefit from the addition of herbs during cooking. Lovage is a useful herb for vegetarian loaves and hot-pots as it adds a yeasty, almost meaty flavour.

CARROTS WITH SALAD BURNET

Carrots
Butter
Freshly ground black pepper
Salad burnet leaves—generous quantities

1. Slice carrots thinly and steam until slightly soft.
2. Add butter, freshly ground black pepper and burnet leaves and mix together until the butter has melted. Serve immediately.

COURGETTES AND TOMATOES WITH BASIL

Tomatoes
Courgettes
Vegetable oil for frying
Chives and basil, chopped finely
Freshly ground black pepper

1. Place the tomatoes in boiling water for a few minutes until the skins split, then cool them quickly under running water. Remove the skins and chop the tomatoes.
2. Fry the courgettes in vegetable oil for a few minutes. Add the remaining ingredients, cover the pan and simmer for about 5 minutes until the courgettes are just tender.

VEGETABLE LOAF

½ cup red or green lentils, cooked
1 large onion, finely chopped
2 small carrots, grated
1 stick celery, finely chopped
1 small turnip or parsnip, grated
2 oz (55g) wholemeal breadcrumbs
Sea salt and freshly ground black pepper
Parsley, lovage and thyme, finely chopped
1 large egg, beaten

1. Place the lentils, vegetables, breadcrumbs, seasoning and herbs in a mixing bowl and bind together with the beaten egg.
2. Place the mixture in a greased loaf tin and bake at 350°F/180°C (Gas Mark 4) for 30 minutes.

SWEET DISHES

Herbs are not usually associated with sweet dishes, but nevertheless there are some which have a definite affinity with fruit or creamy desserts. Elderflowers, mint and the leaves of lemon or rose-scented geraniums can be used as the base for subtly flavoured creams and sorbets. Lemon thyme can be sprinkled over fruit salad and a sprig of rosemary baked in a rice pudding. Leaves of sweet herbs like angelica and sweet cicely are often stewed with fruit—especially rhubarb and gooseberries—so that less sugar is needed.

HERB CREAM

1 pint (570ml) milk
2 tablespoons milk powder
3–4 tablespoons rice flour
8 sprigs lemon thyme or
*   4 sprigs rosemary*
2 egg whites, whipped
4 tablespoons double cream, whipped

1. Place the milk in a saucepan, add milk powder, rice flour and herbs and bring to the boil slowly, stirring all the time.
2. Cook for a few minutes and then allow to cool thoroughly.
3. Remove the herbs and fold in the whipped egg whites and cream. Serve chilled, sprinkled with toasted nuts or with fruit.

GOOSEBERRIES WITH SWEET CICELY

Gooseberries
Sweet cicely, chopped or whole fresh leaves
Honey to taste

1. Simmer the fruit and herbs until tender. Remove the whole leaves after cooking; chopped ones left in the fruit add a mild aniseed flavour.
2. Add honey to taste and serve.

BREAD, BISCUITS AND SCONES

Herb flavoured bread, biscuits and scones are particularly useful for livening up a snack meal. They take advantage of the strength and nutty texture of some herb seeds: caraway seeds are not to everyone's liking, but lovage seeds make a pleasant savoury bread—one which will complement a plain cheese or a herb cheese. Dried and fresh herb leaves can also be used in baking—but relatively large quantities are needed. Fresh herbs are best in light cheese scones, served on their own, warmed and spread with butter, as a savoury snack.

DARK LOVAGE BREAD

1 oz (30g) fresh yeast or ¹/₂oz (15g) dried
2 teaspoons molasses, malt extract or Barbados sugar
¹/₂ pint (285ml) tepid water
1 lb (455g) wholemeal flour
1 tablespoon vegetable oil
1 tablespoon lovage seeds (or to taste)

1. Activate the yeast with the molasses in ¼ pint (140ml) water.
2. Mix the flour with the oil and lovage seeds. Add the yeast mixture and remaining water to make a dough and knead well.
3. Put into an oiled bread tin and leave in a warm place until well risen.
4. Bake in a hot oven, 400°F/200°C (Gas Mark 6) for about 45 minutes.

SWEET ROSEMARY BISCUITS

4 oz (115g) butter
2 oz (55g) raw cane sugar or honey
6 oz (170g) wholemeal flour
2 tablespoons fresh or dried rosemary, finely chopped

1. Cream the butter and raw cane sugar or honey.
2. Add the flour and rosemary and knead the mixture well.
3. Turn out onto a floured board, roll out and cut into rounds.
4. Bake for about 10 minutes at 400°F/200°C (Gas Mark 6).

HERB SCONES

¹/₂lb (225g) wholemeal flour
1 teaspoon bicarbonate of soda
2 oz (55g) butter or polyunsaturated margarine
2 oz (55g) grated cheese
¼ pint (140ml) natural yogurt
Mixed fresh chopped herbs, e.g. parsley, tarragon, chives, pot marjoram

1. Mix flour and bicarbonate of soda and rub in the butter or polyunsaturated margarine.
2. Stir in the remaining ingredients and knead to form a soft dough.
3. Roll about ¾ inch (2cm) thick and cut into rounds.
4. Place on a greased baking tray and bake at 425°F/220°C (Gas Mark 7) for about 15 minutes.

HERB BUTTERS AND PRESERVES

There are many ways of adding a herb flavour to a dish—use herb butters for garnishing and sandwiches, oils and vinegars for salad dressings, jellies and pickles to serve with salad and cheese.

CHIVE BUTTER

3 oz (85g) butter
3 tablespoons chopped chives
1 tablespoon lemon juice

1. Allow butter to soften at room temperature.
2. Mix in chopped chives and lemon juice with a fork.
3. Chill until wanted for use.

BASIL AND GARLIC OIL

Basil leaves to loosely fill a
  3/4-pint measure
3/4 pint (425ml) mild-flavoured oil
1 clove garlic, halved
2 chilli peppers

1. Bruise basil leaves lightly and put them in a wide-necked jar.
2. Cover with oil and leave in a cold, dark place for one month.
3. Strain into a bottle and drop in the garlic, chilli peppers and a small fresh sprig of basil. Seal tightly.

DILL PICKLING VINEGAR

1/2 pint (300ml) white wine vinegar
1 dill flower-head
1 sprig tarragon

2 tablespoons pickling spice
1 tablespoon grated horseradish root

1. Put the vinegar, dill, tarragon and spices in a covered basin standing in a saucepan of water.
2. Bring the water to a boil, remove from the heat, and leave the ingredients to infuse for 2 hours.
3. Add the grated horseradish when cool, and put into jars.
4. This recipe can be used to preserve gherkins, onions or cauliflower florets. Add fresh dill flower-heads to the jars for effect.

LEMON THYME AND APPLE JELLY

2 lb (900g) cooking apples
1 lb (455g) raw cane sugar for every
  1 pint (570ml) liquid
3 sprigs fresh lemon thyme or
  2 teaspoons dried to every
  1 pint (570ml) liquid

1. Wash and cut up the apples. Cover with water and boil until soft.
2. Pour into a jelly bag, drain overnight, measure the level of liquid and weigh the correct amount of sugar.
3. Place the liquid in a pan, add herbs (tying dried herbs in a piece of muslin) and boil for 10 minutes.
4. Add sugar and continue boiling until the setting point is reached.
5. Remove the herbs and pour the jelly into jars. Stir in a sprinkling of fresh thyme leaves and seal.

CHAPTER 10
HERB TEAS AND DRINKS

Herbs can be used in a variety of refreshing drinks, hot and cold: fruit cups, alcoholic punches, milk-based drinks and China tea. However, they are of most value when used on their own to make herb teas: some are relaxing, others stimulating—and each has its own distinctive but delicate flavour. You can pick one to suit your every mood.

Garden design

Figure 26 shows a small circular garden of herbs that are popular for drinks and herb teas—but other personal favourites could be substituted. The central feature is a pot of lemon verbena which must be moved to a greenhouse or conservatory during the winter. All the plants are attractive ones, and there is plenty of colour from the flowers of borage (blue), chamomile (white) and bergamot (red).

Cold drinks

Borage and mint (spearmint or peppermint) are attractive for iced summer drinks and seem to impart a coolness of their own: try young leaves steeped in clear apple juice or in a punch based on cider or white wine. Strain them out after a few hours and add fresh sprigs of mint or borage flowers for decoration.

Elderflowers give a delightful heady fragrance to home-made lemonade: simply steep two or three flowerheads and a sliced lemon in 1 pint (570ml)

water for a few hours; strain and sweeten with a little honey. Elderflowers have a natural yeast on them and will make a spontaneously sparkling 'champagne' ideal for a special picnic.

ELDERFLOWER CHAMPAGNE

6 large elderflower heads
1 gallon (4.5 litres) water
1 lb (455g) sugar
1 lemon, sliced
2 tablespoons wine vinegar

1. Mix the ingredients in a wine bucket, cover and leave in a warm place for two or three days.
2. Strain and pour into screw-top bottles.
3. Tighten the caps of the bottles a few days before the champagne is to be drunk to allow the 'sparkle' to build up.

Herb teas

A sprig of mint or lemon balm added to a cup of ordinary black tea will give it an additional subtle flavour. However, many herbs make delicious teas on their own: bergamot tastes similar to a fine China tea and is an excellent one to try first; lemon balm, lemon verbena and lemon thyme all have easily acquired tastes, as do spearmint, apple mint and peppermint. Some of these pleasurable herb teas have therapeutic properties: lemon balm and chamomile, for example, both make particularly soothing drinks.

As in cooking, the quantities needed

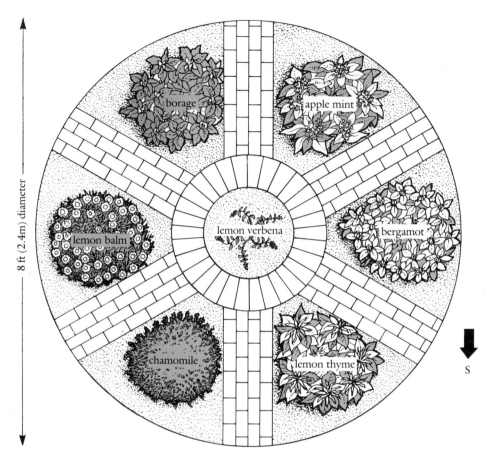

8 ft (2.4m) diameter

borage

apple mint

lemon balm

lemon verbena

bergamot

chamomile

lemon thyme

S

Figure 26 Design for a herb tea garden.

depend on the quality of the herbs and individual taste. As a general guide, use a couple of medium-sized fresh leaves of herbs like mint (or a small sprig of those like thyme) for each cup. Simply put the leaves in the cup and pour on boiling water. With dried herbs use about ½ a teaspoon per person and treat the brew in the same way as ordinary tea. If possible keep a china teapot specially for

herb teas as their delicate flavour can easily be tainted. Cover the cups or pot and allow the herbs to steep for about five minutes. Stronger brews are usually required for medicinal teas (see Chapter 11), and it may not be wise to drink these in large quantities or consistently over a period of several months. Check the herb in Chapter 11 and in a good herbal if you are uncertain.

CHAPTER 11
THE MEDICINAL AND COSMETIC HERB GARDEN

Even some common garden herbs contain powerful healing substances, and anyone can learn to use these plants to treat minor ailments at home. However, they should *not* be considered just as natural drugs, to substitute for the chemist's aspirins and ointments: they are far more than this. Incorporating herbs into your daily diet, and judicious use of herbal remedies to help the body heal itself, can keep you healthy in a way that pills never can. Beauty relies as much on diet and health as on creams and lotions, thus cosmetic herbs and medicinal herbs are inseparable—a fact that will take you more and more often to the herb garden rather than to the chemist's shop!

Garden design
A few of the best medicinal herbs are shrubs and others are tall, rampant growers so the medicinal herb garden should allow space for these. The garden design shown in Figure 27 puts blackberries and elderberries against a back wall and tall mullein plants along a side wall. Hops are trained over an arbour and raspberries along wires as in a fruit cage, to screen the herb garden. Several of the medicinal herbs are natives of damp places, so a shallow pond or boggy area has been created in the garden where these can be planted (see pages 28-29); they do well in partial shade. The garden has a solid centrepiece—a pot, pillar or statue.

Principles of herbal medicine
The herbalist's approach is different from that of conventional modern medicine in ways that it is helpful to understand, even when all you are considering is using a few herbs from the garden to keep you healthy and treat minor ailments. The body (and mind) must be treated as a whole—rather than as parts to which drugs can be specifically directed. It is not the symptoms but their underlying cause which must be treated. For example, indigestion is often caused by nervous tension, and in such a case a herb with digestive and relaxant properties (like hops), together with an attempt to remove the cause of tension, would be a far better remedy than indigestion tablets.

In most cases of minor illness the body will correct *itself* given a chance, and the symptoms are often the signs of it throwing off the disease: diarrhoea, for example, is the body's defence against intestinal infection.

Herbal remedies work alongside these natural body processes rather than suppressing them as modern drugs so often do: yarrow, for example, will reduce a fever by promoting sweating and moving blood to the skin. This also explains why many herbs treat ailments with opposite symptoms: elderberries and elderflowers will help both diarrhoea and constipation because of the regulating effect they have on the bowels.

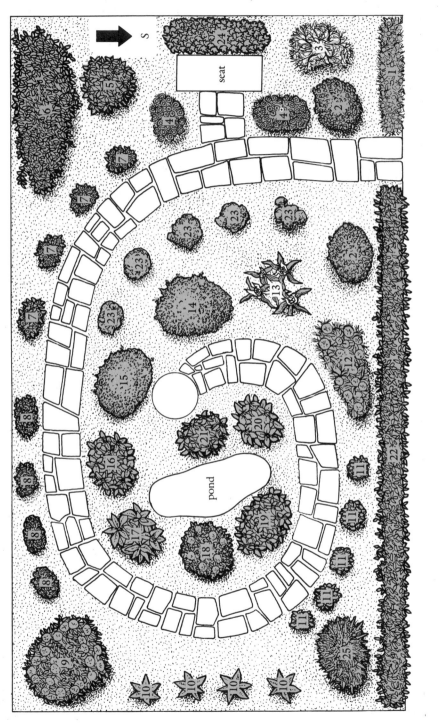

Figure 27 Design for a medicinal herb garden.
Key: 1 dill; 2 lady's mantle; 3 fennel; 4 chamomile; 5 rosemary; 6 blackberry; 7 pot marigolds; 8 feverfew; 9 elder; 10 mullein; 11 heartsease pansies; 12 yarrow; 13 garlic; 14 garden thyme; 15 lemon thyme; 16 sage; 17 horseradish; 18 meadowsweet; 19 peppermint; 20 lemon balm; 21 comfrey; 22 raspberries; 23 parsley; 24 hops; 25 lavender.

Many orthodox drugs were originally extracted from herbs, although most of these are now synthesized. However, in herbal medicine it is important to use the plant itself rather than an isolated active ingredient, because its other constituents also play a vital role. They often enhance the beneficial action of the herb or act as buffers so that no unwanted side effects occur. This can be seen in the action of meadowsweet. This herb contains salicylic compounds—like those contained in aspirins—and can similarly be used to reduce pain. With aspirins these active compounds cause temporary damage to the stomach walls: meadowsweet, on the other hand, also contains mucilages which protect the stomach from harmful effects.

Preparation and use of herbal remedies

Although herbs recommended for home use are usually quite safe—often more so than the drugs on the chemist's counter—there are a few precautions that you should take before treating yourself.

1. You should only treat *minor* illnesses—if you are unsure of the symptoms see a doctor or qualified herbalist.

2. If you are picking the herb fresh from the garden or the wild make sure you have identified it correctly—check in a book and with someone who is knowledgeable about herbs, if at all possible.

3. If the remedy is an unusual one that you have been told or have read about, cross-check it.

4. It is unwise to take some herbs consistently in large doses and/or over many weeks. Switch to another recommended herb for a time if you are not sure.

5. Be aware that certain conditions—pregnancy, for example—may mean that an otherwise appropriate herbal remedy is unsafe.

To prescribe exact doses of herbal medicines is meaningless because, as in cookery, the quality of herbs varies and so does their effect on different individuals. General guidelines are given here and these can be modified by experience.

The commonest and simplest way to administer a herb is as a tea or *infusion* of the dried leaves: the normal strength is one ounce of dried herbs to one pint of boiling water (30g to 500ml) or one heaped teaspoonful per cup. For roots and seeds, however, it is usually necessary to make a *decoction* by simmering them in water for about twenty minutes.

Herbalists often use *tinctures*, which are alcoholic extracts of the herb which can be taken from a bottle almost like conventional medicine. At home, tinctures can be made for some herbs with a cheap wine, and can be a convenient way of preserving the fresh plant (see page 59). Dried herbs are more often used, however: add 1 part herb to 4–5 parts wine and leave to macerate for about two weeks before straining off the liquid. Surgical spirit can be used as the base if the tincture is for external use.

An easy way to apply herbs to a swelling or inflammation is to use a *compress*—a bandage soaked in a thick infusion or decoction. Alternatively a *poultice* can be made by sewing leaves or finely chopped roots in a muslin bag and soaking this in a bowl of boiling water; apply it to the skin as soon as it is cool enough.

Oils are good for massaging aches and pains and skin care, almond oil being the best base (see page 58). Ointments can similarly be made by infusing the herb in melted lanolin.

Herbs in a healthy diet

Including small amounts of herbs regularly in the daily diet can be a positive benefit to health in several ways. Eaten raw in salads, many herbs provide valuable amounts of vitamins and minerals. Morever, they provide these elements in a way in which they can be easily absorbed. Parsley, for example, is particularly high in iron, vitamin C, vitamin A, calcium, phosphorus and manganese; the vitamin C helps the body absorb the iron (making fresh parsley ideal for someone who is anaemic, and more effective than simple iron tablets in some cases). Other constituents of herbs help the body to function well: the circulation, digestion, and elimination of waste.

Finally, using herbs in cooking can reduce the need for harmful additives and prevent over-use of salt and sugar: they provide flavour and interest which certainly make ketchups redundant! Similarly herb teas can replace the less-than-healthy cups of coffee and tea that we drink.

Herbs for common ailments

The following herbs are pleasant and safe to take for treating yourself at home—but remember they only work by helping the body to help itself, so do not expect instant results. You must also help by resting, eating correctly and taking any other appropriate measures to ensure recovery.

Feverish colds

Yarrow—reduces fever; particularly good when stomach problems are a cause because it has a calming effect. Use a normal strength tea as required, but with caution in pregnancy.

Elderflower—reduces fever; good when chestiness is also a problem as it will help relieve congestion. Use normal strength tea as required—very safe.

Coughs, sore throat and mouth

Thyme—will counteract infections of throat and lungs and also calm the muscles there—particularly good for a dry cough. Use normal strength tea or gargle three to four times a day.

Mullein—will clear the lungs by stimulating a cough but, because it contains mucilage, will also soothe any soreness. The flowers are more effective than the leaves. Use normal strength tea as required.

Sage—acts as a disinfectant in the mouth and throat, and reduces catarrh. Use half the normal strength i.e. ½ oz in 1 pint water (15g in 500ml) as tea or gargle, two or three times a day.

Blackberry leaves—soothe and heal mouth ulcers, bleeding gums and sore throats. Normal strength decoction as a drink or gargle when required.

Poor circulation

Horseradish—increases blood flow to counteract feeling of 'chill' in illness; good for poor circulation and chilblains. Use the fresh root only in the amounts you can happily eat: as horseradish sauce, or as a tincture of the fresh root in vodka. Do not make a tea or decoction, or use in cases of stomach ulcers or very high blood-pressure.

Garlic—increases blood flow; good for varicose veins; also lowers the blood-pressure and the level of cholesterol in the blood so is helpful to those with high blood-pressure. Dose is anything up to three raw cloves a day.

Indigestion, sickness, constipation and diarrhoea

Chamomile—has a calming effect on the digestive system, thus is particularly good for nervous indigestion. Use normal strength tea of the flowers as required—a very safe remedy.

Meadowsweet—counteracts stomach acidity, moderates diarrhoea and has a soothing action. Use normal strength tea as required.

Peppermint—is an immediate comfort for all stomach pains and nausea. Use normal strength tea as required but do not use continuously for prolonged periods.

Hops—have a relaxing effect on the digestive system and their bitterness stimulates the appetite. Use normal strength tea, one cup twice a day, but do not use for prolonged periods or in cases of depression.

Fennel and dill—are carminatives, particularly good for indigestion and colic (they are the basis of gripe water used for babies). Use the seeds to make a normal strength decoction and take one tablespoon three times a day. Do not use stronger doses and avoid during pregnancy.

Sage, garlic and thyme—have an antibiotic effect when an infection is the cause of the trouble.

Tension, sleeplessness, headaches

Lemon balm—one of the best relaxing and tranquillizing herbs and one that is very safe. Use normal strength tea as required.

Hops—a mild sedative (see above for dose).

Meadowsweet—can be used as a painkiller to support to another herbal remedy (see above for dose).

Feverfew—used as meadowsweet, for headaches in particular, and may be a more effective remedy for some people. Use normal strength tea, one or two cups a day, or eat one or two small fresh leaves in a sandwich.

Skin complaints, bruises, wounds and cuts

Comfrey—has an important healing effect on damaged tissues: cuts, bruises and strains. Use a poultice or compress, or an oil if the wound is not open.

Thyme—use as a disinfectant for washing wounds.

Pot marigold—helps stop bleeding and is mildly antiseptic, thus is good for cuts; it will also reduce skin inflammations. Use the flowers to make a poultice, compress, oil or ointment.

Heartsease and parsley—internal cleansing herbs particularly useful for skin complaints that are caused by toxins in the body. Use normal strength tea as required.

Women's complaints

Raspberry leaves—ease period pains; good in pregnancy. Normal strength tea, two small cups a day.

Lady's mantle—may help any menstrual disorders. Use normal strength tea, two small cups a day.

Fennel—stimulates menstrual flow (see above for dose).

Cosmetic preparations

Healthy and attractive skin, hair and nails will only come with good general health, helped by a diet including herbs and herbal remedies as described in the previous sections. However, herbal cosmetics provide a valuable back-up, utilizing the medicinal properties of the herbs, such as their astringency or relaxing effect, as well as their lovely scents. With a little effort, you can avoid all shop-bought products, replacing them with home-made preparations that contain only natural ingredients like eggs, oatmeal, glycerine, arrowroot and vegetable oils. A few of the simplest ideas are described here.

Bath herbs

Tie sprigs of fresh herbs in a bunch under the hot water tap while the bath is running, or use dried herbs mixed with oatmeal in a muslin bag. Different herbs produce different effects. Try choosing from the following:

Lavender or eau-de-cologne mint—for scent

Chamomile, elder—soothing and healing for minor skin complaints and inflammation.

Chamomile, lemon balm—relaxing.

Lemon thyme, yarrow—astringent, invigorating.

Hair rinses

Rinse the hair with a herbal infusion after shampooing and washing away the soap. Use about four tablespoons of the dried herb to 1 pint (500ml) of boiling water and allow to cool until lukewarm. Choose one to suit your type of hair:

Chamomile, pot marigold—to lighten and condition blonde hair.

Rosemary, sage—to condition dark hair.

Yarrow with peppermint—for dandruff and hair loss.

Skin conditioners

An infusion of a soothing herb like pot marigold in almond oil makes a good conditioner for dry skin. For oily skin, an infusion in water of an astringent herb like yarrow makes a good cleanser.

CHAPTER 12
THE POT-POURRI GARDEN

In summer, the pot-pourri garden is a place to sit and enjoy the flowers, the scents and the insects at work. The herbs that are grown will make pot-pourri mixtures with their own subtle fragrance, bringing memories of the sunshine into dark winter days. Some dried herb mixtures can also be used to scent linen and keep the clothes moths away, whilst others can be put in herb cushions and pillows where their relaxing effect is particularly appreciated.

Garden design

Providing leaves and flowers for pot-pourri gives the opportunity to grow some of the most attractive and beautifully scented herbs: some with colourful flowers, others with variegated foliage, and many that are beloved by bees and butterflies. A sheltered spot and a place to sit are essentials, and as many of the most suitable plants are climbers, walls or arches to support them are useful.

Figure 28 shows a design around which straight borders, one either side of a garden path, could easily be planned. A south wall provides shelter and supports roses, jasmine and honeysuckle. The borders are divided into semicircles by brick paths. One space is paved and contains a seat and space for pots of tender herbs like bay and lemon verbena. Scented geraniums are bedded out in the opposite bed. This and the other two beds to the north of the path contain the other hardy and half-hardy

annuals; all of these are relatively low-growing so they do not create much shade. Lavender and hyssop form flowering hedges along the full length of the path. Although the plan is for a fairly large garden, the number and size of the semicircles and the variety of plants could be adapted to one of any dimension.

Pot-pourri ingredients

Pot-pourri is basically a blend of scented flowers and leaves, but other ingredients are usually added. These include ground spices, dried orange and lemon peel, and sometimes spirits like brandy and concentrated scented oils. Nearly all mixtures include a 'fixative'— a substance which helps the pot-pourri keep its fragrance by holding and blending the oils from the herbs.

Leaves and flowers

There are many varied herbs and flowers to choose from, as indicated in Table 12. Leaves may have recognizable perfumes like lavender and eau-de-Cologne mint; they may have an indefinable sweetness like pineapple sage and pineapple mint, or the spiciness of sweet marjoram and bay. The seeds of coriander and caraway can be ground and used instead of the exotic spices cinnamon, cloves, and nutmeg which are often called for in recipes. Herbs like red bergamot add both to the scent and appearance of a mixture,

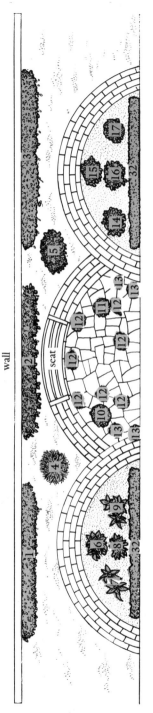
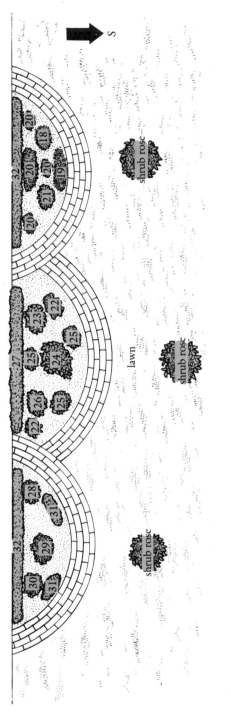

Figure 28 Design for a pot-pourri garden.

Key: 1 honeysuckle; 2 climbing rose; 3 jasmine; 4 southernwood; 5 rosemary; 6 costmary; 7 Florentine iris; 8 alkanet; 9 bergamot; 10 bay (in pot); 11 lemon verbena (in pot); 12 pinks; 13 grape hyacinths; 14 pineapple mint; 15 peppermint; 16 anise hyssop; 17 eau-de-Cologne mint; 18 cotton lavender; 19 double chamomile; 20 pot marigolds; 21 curry plant; 22 cornflowers; 23 rose geranium; 24 pineapple sage; 25 pansies; 26 lemon geranium; 27 hyssop hedge (blue and pink flowers); 28 sweet marjoram; 29 thymes; 30 basils.

Table 12: Flowers and leaves for pot-pourri

Scented leaves	Scented flowers	Flowers for colour
Anise hyssop (sweet aniseed scent)	Bergamot (red)	Alkanet (blue)
Basil (spicy)	Chamomile, double (white)	Borage (blue)
Bay (spicy)	Honeysuckle (predominately pink)	Cornflowers (blues and pinks)
Bergamot	Jasmine (white)	Curry plant (yellow)
Chamomile (sweet)	Lavender (blue and pink)	Grape hyacinths (blue)
Eau-de-Cologne mint	Pinks (pink and white)	Marigolds (yellow)
Geraniums (scented)	Roses (all colours)	Pansies (all colours)
Lemon verbena	Violets (blue and white)	
Peppermint		
Pineapple mint (sweet scent)		
Pineapple sage (sweet scent)		
Rosemary		
Sweet marjoram (spicy)		
Thymes—garden thyme, lemon thyme, and other sweetly scented thymes		

but sometimes extra colour must be provided by flowers which have no appreciable smell: marigolds, cornflowers or pansies, for example. Rose petals are the traditional basis for many pot-pourri mixtures; the old-fashioned shrub roses are highly scented but as they are large and flower only for a short time, they are often not suitable for growing in the herb garden. Some of the less vigorous scented climbers are easier to incorporate (see pages 25 and 27).

Fixatives

One of the commonest fixatives used in pot-pourri today is orris-root powder. This should be easy to buy, but you can also make it yourself because it comes from the dried and ground-up rhizomes of the white-flowered iris *Iris florentina*. Orris-root powder has a pleasantly sweet perfume of its own, and this must be taken into consideration when adding it to mixtures. There are other 'home-grown' fixatives, but none are particularly easy to prepare: angelica root, for example, which must also be dried and ground before use. The powdered resin 'gum benzoin' is the other fixative frequently mentioned in recipes; this should be available from specialist suppliers. Salt is used in making some particular types of pot-pourri; where possible use sea salt or pure rock salt with no chemical additives.

Aromatic oils

Concentrated oils—like the familiar oil of peppermint and oil of lavender which are sold in most chemists—are extracts of aromatic herbal oils, usually obtained from the plants by distillation. Many such oils are available from specialist suppliers, popular ones being oils of bergamot, rose, and geranium. Most of them are very expensive, but very strong—only a few drops are called for in most pot-pourri recipes. They are used to strengthen the scent of the mixtures and are widely used in shop-bought products. In home-made pot-pourris they should be used with extreme caution—only added a drop at a time—or they will drown the subtle fragrance of the other ingredients. If the mixture contains enough fragrant flowers and leaves, their use can be avoided altogether. Oils can also be used to revive a mixture whose scent is fading, but with a pot-pourri garden to pick from it is more fun to start again!

Pot-pourri methods and mixtures

There are two basic types of pot-pourri: one 'dry' and the other 'moist'. Dry pot-pourri is made with leaves and flowers collected throughout the season and dried as described on pages 56-7. These are mixed with a fixative, and with ground spices and aromatic oils if required. When being used, dry pot-pourri is generally put into open bowls or glass containers and it is for this type of mixture that colourful flowers are important. 'Moist' pot-pourri uses fresh flowers and leaves, which are dried just until they are limp; they are then put into a crock with layers of salt and left to cake, before the fixative and other ingredients like spices, oils and spirits (which keep the mixture moist) are added. Moist pot-pourris are said to have richer more lasting scents, but they are neither so pretty nor so easy to make as dry mixtures.

There are no strict rules for pot-pourri making: combinations and quantities are a matter of personal preference best determined by trial and error. The following simple mixtures can easily be adapted according to what you have growing. As a rough guide, the amount of orris-root needed as a fixative is approximately one tablespoon of the powder to about six cups of dried petals and leaves. Spices are used in about the same amounts and aromatic oils at the rate of not more than one drop to every cup of petals.

LAVENDER AND MINT POT-POURRI

3 cups dried lavender flowers
1 cup dried peppermint leaves
1/2 cup dried purple basil
1/2 cup dried rosemary
1 tablespoon orris-root powder

Gently combine all the ingredients in a bowl. Extra flowers can be added for colour—choose blue or purple ones like pansies and cornflowers. Cover the bowl tightly (cling film is good for this) and leave it in a dry, dark, warm place for a week, stirring daily, to allow the scents to blend.

SPICY LEMON POT-POURRI

1 cup dried lemon verbena leaves
1 cup dried lemon thyme
4 cups dried rose petals (yellow or white)
Dried grated rind of 1 lemon
1 tablespoon orris-root powder
1/2 tablespoon ground coriander
1/2 tablespoon ground bay leaf

Combine the ingredients as above. Suitable flowers to add include chamomile and marigold.

ROSE AND BERGAMOT POT-POURRI

3 cups dried red rose petals
1 cup dried rose-scented geranium leaves
1 cup bergamot leaves and flowers
1 tablespoon orris-root powder

Combine the ingredients as above.

When the pot-pourri mixtures are ready they should be tipped into attractive containers. These should have tight-fitting lids so that they can be sealed to retain the fragrance when they are not in use. Wide-necked kitchen jars with cork stoppers are good; and suitable and sometimes unusual bowls and jars can often be found in second-hand shops.

Herb sachets, cushions and pillows

Dried herb mixtures can be used to stuff small sachets for placing amongst clothes and linen. Use muslin or fine cotton to hold the filling and cover this with a thin attractive outer cover if you wish. Herbs reputed to keep moths away are some of the harsher smelling ones like hyssop, cotton lavender, southernwood and wormwood, but these can be mixed with sweeter herbs like lavender, rosemary and mints to give a scent far preferable to that of moth-balls.

Large flat herb sachets can be slipped inside a cushion or pillow, where they will emit a pleasant fragrance when crushed. Popular herbs for cushion mixtures include lavender, rosemary, lemon verbena, thyme and bergamot; use a fixative as for pot-pourri if you want the fragrance to last. For herb pillows choose delicately scented herbs: hops and lemon balm are particularly valuable because they are relaxing herbs whose effect can actually work directly through our noses!

CHAPTER 13

HERBS ON THE PATIO

Herbs are ideal plants for growing in containers on a patio or in a sunny back yard. Many will stand up well to the often hot and dry conditions, and form bushy plants that are attractive as well as useful. Pots of the strong aromatic herbs can supply the kitchen throughout the summer, and even some salad and tea herbs will produce useful amounts of foliage, conveniently to hand.

Which herbs to grow

The best herbs to grow are thus the dry-leaved sun loving herbs like rosemary, sage, sweet marjoram, savories and thymes. Garden thyme and lemon thyme are the most useful, but the dwarf creeping thymes with their colourful foliage and pretty flowers will fill in the gaps, trail over trough edges and spill out of the holes in strawberry pots (see Figure 29). Scented geraniums also make excellent pot plants and the lemon-scented *Pelargonium graveolens* and peppermint-scented *Pelargonium tormentosum* will trail from tubs and hanging baskets.

Lusher herbs like basil, parsley, chives, salad burnet and the mints can be equally successful, but will need more attention. Even some of the tall clumpy herbs like sorrel, lovage and fennel can be grown if they are kept cut: once the clumps fill the pots, plenty of leafy growth will be produced at their base. For tarragon, grow the French rather than the Russian variety as this will form a more compact plant. Bay trees closely clipped to cone or mushroom shapes are particularly suitable for a formal setting, and lemon verbena plants can also be trained as standards although they never form a tight bush.

Herbs which do not do well in pots are the deep-rooted moisture-loving ones like angelica, sweet cicely, comfrey, meadowsweet and horseradish.

Choosing and planting containers

A collection of individual flower pots will make a simple but effective herb 'garden' on a patio (Figure 30). In some ways they are preferable to large tubs or window boxes because they can be easily moved; each herb can be given the growing conditions it needs and sickly plants can be substituted without disturbing the rest. Clay pots are less likely to blow over or become waterlogged than plastic ones, as well as being more attractive. Six-inch (15cm) pots are large enough for the aromatic herbs like thyme and rosemary, but eight-inch (20cm) ones would allow parsley, chives, salad burnet and the mints to produce more useful quantities of foliage.

Old sinks and troughs, wooden boxes and half-barrels, and large clay pots are all good for collections of herbs; try to plant up each container with a group of herbs which like the same growing conditions (Figure 31). All containers should have drainage holes, and in ones that are deep, a layer of 'crock' (broken pots) or rough gravel should be put in the bottom to help prevent waterlogging.

All containers must be filled with a good growing medium. This needs to contain plant foods and also retain moisture. Ordinary garden soil on its own is not suitable because it packs down hard and does not allow air to the plant roots. The soil-based (*John Innes*) and peat-based potting 'composts' on sale in garden shops are expensive and all contain chemicals. An organic-soil based mixture suitable for herb growing can be made with the following ingredients:

4 parts good garden soil
3 parts well-rotted garden compost
3 parts moist peat
1 part horticultural sand

For lush herbs such as parsley and mints, mix in a small amount of a general organic fertilizer like blood, fish and bonemeal: use about 1oz (30g) to a two gallon (10 litre) bucketful. Comfrey leaves can be used instead of either the garden compost or the fertilizer as they are an excellent source of plant nutrients (see page 91). However, this does mean preparing your mixture in advance—ideally in the autumn before spring planting. Simply mix equal amounts of moist peat and chopped comfrey in a polythene sack, tie the top and leave it in a shed or garage over winter. By spring the comfrey will have completely broken down and its sticky residues will have been absorbed by the peat. Mix this with soil and sand as above.

Spring and early summer are the best times for planting container gardens. Make sure both the soil mixture and the plants are thoroughly moist before planting. Afterwards keep the herbs

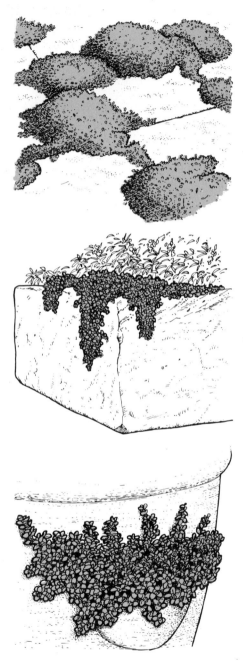

Figure 29 Creeping thymes in the patio garden: between paving stones, trailing over trough edges and in strawberry pots.

Figure 30 Culinary herbs grown in individual pots on a patio, from left to right: garden thyme, chives, parsley, rosemary, French tarragon, pot marjoram.

well watered, and in the shade if it is hot, until they have become established.

Care of the container garden

Like herbs growing in the garden, pot-grown plants must have sunshine: as much as possible in early spring and not too much in mid-summer. The advantage of pots is that they can be moved around to satisfy the conditions that each herb needs. For example, parsley, mints and chives should be kept in semi-shade during the summer months, whereas thymes, rosemary and sage like full sun except during very hot spells.

Watering is most important, particularly for the lusher herbs: in summer, check that the soil mixture in the pots is moist each day—even after rain, because thick foliage can prevent moisture from reaching the roots. Spray the leaves with a watering can in the morning or evening during hot dry spells. In spring and autumn, over watering can cause problems with the aromatic herbs: water only if the soil mixture in the pots becomes dry.

The key to keeping the herbs fresh and attractive is regular clipping and regular feeding, to encourage new growth. In summer use a liquid comfrey feed (see page 91) or one of the proprietary brands of liquid feed—there are one or two organic ones available. Water with this once a week for the lusher herbs and once a fortnight for the aromatic herbs. In autumn and spring when the plants are not growing so strongly, use a liquid seaweed solution. Start feeding newly planted herbs after they have been in their pots about six weeks.

The disadvantage of using a home-made potting medium is that it will contain weed seeds (shop-bought 'potting compost' is sterilized). Do not let any weeds establish themselves in the herb pots—there is no room for competition!

In winter, plants in pots are more susceptible to frost and to waterlogging than those in the garden. The half-hardy perennials should be brought into a light frost-free place and ideally the other pots should be given some protection as well. It is possible to keep many of them green throughout the winter on a kitchen windowsill but there is rarely enough light for them; the slow lank growth which results is scarcely useful—and seems to be very attractive to aphids. However, although herbs kept in a cold greenhouse or conservatory will die down in winter, they will have a head start in the spring and provide welcome fresh greenery.

Figure 31 A collection of different varieties of sage in a large terracotta pot.

CHAPTER 14
HERBS AROUND THE GARDEN

Herbs can be as useful in the garden as they are in the house. In the kitchen garden, herb plants can have a beneficial effect on the fruit and vegetable crops as well as supplying more foliage for cutting and drying. Many will look good in a flower border and provide material for flower arrangements as well as extra for pot-pourri. Herbal brews can be used on fruit, vegetables and flowers, as natural substitutes for chemical fertilizers, pesticides and fungicides.

Herbs grown in the vegetable garden
The vegetable garden often provides space for extra culinary herbs—those used in quantity like parsley, sorrel and garlic or needed for seed such as dill and lovage. But sometimes they are grown directly for the benefit of the crops, as 'companion plants'. This practice seems to be the subject of more old wives' tales than any other gardening topic! Do cabbages really do better when interplanted with thyme or dill, and do broad beans interspersed with summer savory suffer less from blackfly?

Individual gardeners have frequently reported success with these aromatic companionships, but there is little scientific evidence to back them up. However, some pests—like carrot fly— do find their target crops by smelling them out so interplanting with an aromatic herb could help mask the scent. Cabbage root fly identifies brassica plants by their outline against the bare earth, as well as by smell, so here again interplanting could confuse the pest. The other possibility is that some herbs could have a direct effect on crop growth or soil pests through root secretions; there are a few cases where this does happen but, in general, evidence is scarce.

Interplanting is not easy in practice: the crop plant must not be swamped with herbs or vice versa, and since most vegetable crops are cleared and planted in new beds after a season, only the annual herbs really fit in. Garlic could usefully be planted in autumn on the next year's carrot bed or a row of dill sown on the cabbage bed. However, both perennials and annuals should be encouraged to grow on the *edges* of beds and in awkward uncropped corners. For whether or not they directly help a certain crop, they add to the diversity of the garden—and look nice too!

Herbs that attract bees are particularly valuable, as these insects help pollinate fruit, and vegetables such as beans, tomatoes, marrows and cucumbers. Borage is one of the favourite bee herbs and is a large annual which can usefully swamp a weedy spot. The 'labiate' herbs are also popular: the flowers of basil, bergamot, hyssop, marjoram, savory and thyme will always have visiting bees, even in the most inclement weather. So too will flowering chives, which make a good edge to a vegetable

Table 13: Herbs grown for their attractive foliage

Silver/grey herbs	Variegated herbs	Golden herbs	Purple herbs
Cotton lavender *Santolina chamaecyparissus* *Santolina nana* *Santolina neopolitana*	Ginger mint (gold/green) *Mentha gentilis* Lemon balm (green/gold) *Melissa officinalis variegata*	Feverfew *Chrysanthemum parthenium* Golden marjoram *Origanum vulgare* 'aureum'	Bronze fennel *Foeniculum vulgare* 'Bronze' Eau-de-Cologne mint *Mentha citrata*
Curry plant *Helichrysum angustifolium*	Pineapple mint (green/cream) *Mentha rotundifolia variegata*	Golden thyme *Thymus vulgaris aureus*	Purple basil *Ocimum basilicum*
Lavender (most varieties)		Golden hops	Red sage *Salvia officinalis*
Rosemary (most varieties) *Rosmarinus officinalis*	Sage (green/gold) *Salvia officinalis* 'Icterina'	*Humulus lupulus aurea*	'Purpurascens'
Silver thyme *Thymus vulgaris* 'Silver Posie'	Sage (pink/white/green) *Salvia officinalis* 'Tricolor'		
Southernwood *Artemisia abrotanum*			
Wormwood *Artemisia borealis*			

bed. Other beneficial insects may also be attracted by herb plants. Hoverflies, for example will come to flowering Umbellifers such as dill and fennel, and then seek out aphid-infested plants on which to lay their eggs: the larvae which hatch are voracious aphid eaters.

Herbs grown in the flower garden

Similar folklore exists about companion planting in the flower garden: chives, for example, are reputed to prevent black spot on roses and even, somehow, to enhance their smell. The main reason for planting herbs in the flower garden, however, is simply that they are so attractive.

Bergamot is one flowering herb that has long been popular as a herbaceous border plant: as well as the red-flowered 'Cambridge Scarlet' used for herb teas, there are pink- and mauve-flowered varieties. Similarly there are pink and dark purple varieties of lavender. Flowering herbs provide valuable nectar for bees right through from early spring until late summer—and in particular during the first two or three weeks in June when other major sources like fruit blossom can be scarce. Catmint *(Nepeta mussini)* with its clear blue flowers and grey foliage is particularly useful during the early periods, and the decorative mints and marjorams during August and September.

The lasting visual appeal of herbs is as much in their foliage as in their flowers. As Table 13 shows, many common herbs like sage and thyme have golden, purple or variegated varieties. The feathery fronds of bronze fennel provide a useful contrast in the flower border and are excellent in flower arranging, as are the soft round leaves and greeny yellow flowerheads of lady's mantle. Silver-leaved herbs like cotton lavender and many of the *Artemisia* species can be very striking either planted in a mixed border or in a bed of their own.

Herbs as fertilizers, pesticides and fungicides

Herbs are rich in minerals and this property, which makes them such a valuable addition to our own diet, can also benefit our plants. Comfrey is by far the most important in this respect: it is particularly rich in potassium which makes it ideal for feeding fruiting vegetables like tomatoes and cucumbers. It also makes a good general purpose liquid fertilizer, rich enough to supply pot plants and herbs in containers with nutrients. Although the ordinary herbalists' comfrey *(Symphytum officinale)* is adequate for this, the hybrid called 'Russian comfrey' *(Symphytum uplandicum)* contains significantly more potassium, calcium, iron and manganese. It also starts growing earlier in the year and is more vigorous, thus is better for constant cutting.

A quantity of ready-to-use liquid feed for the vegetable garden can be made by filling a water butt loosely with comfrey leaves and then topping it up with water (Figure 32). The comfrey ferments and goes black in about two to four weeks (taking less time in hot weather). The clear brown liquid can then be strained off. A small amount of concentrated feed, convenient for pot plants, can be made by packing leaves tightly into a bucket which has small seep holes in the bottom and weighting them down; the black fermented comfrey juice then gradually drops through and can be collected in a container underneath. Dilute this concentrate at the rate of 2–4 fl oz per gallon (12–25ml per litre).

Comfrey leaves will also act as a good

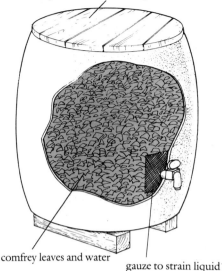

lid to prevent smell and keep out flies

comfrey leaves and water

gauze to strain liquid

Figure 32 Making comfrey liquid fertilizer in a water butt.

'activator' for the compost heap, helping the breakdown of stemmy materials. In fact, *any* left over clippings and debris from the herb garden should be added to the heap as this is the best way of recycling the valuable minerals that they contain, and some may help to activate the heap. The commercially available activator *Quick Return* or QR is of herbal origin, containing juices of chamomile, dandelion, valerian, yarrow and nettle.

Many gardeners have reported success when using herbal brews as pesticides and fungicides: they may not work as immediately or dramatically as chemicals, but neither do they harm wildlife nor leave dangerous residues in the garden. It is hardly surprising that garlic, with its powerful antiseptic properties and high sulphur content seems to make an effective fungicidal spray: soak one crushed clove in a pint (570ml) of water overnight and then strain into the sprayer. The same solution could be used to soak pea and bean seeds before planting to prevent rotting and deter mice.

The strong bitter herbs like wormwood, used as moth repellents in the house, may also act as deterrents to pests in the garden. Try steeping the leaves to make a cold brew as for comfrey, or even scattering the dried herb around the plants. A well-tried insecticide and fungicide can be made from elder leaves: by simmering about 1lb in 4 pints of water (455g in 2.2 litres) for 30 minutes. It has been reported to be particularly effective against mildew and blackspot on roses.

CHAPTER 15
GROWING INFORMATION FOR INDIVIDUAL HERBS

In this chapter, about fifty of the most useful and easiest-to-grow herbs are listed in alphabetical order. For each herb it gives:

Varieties—ones that are commonly found in catalogues (see pages 11-12 for an explanation of names).

Description—whether the herb is annual or perennial, hardy or half-hardy, herbaceous or shrubby, deciduous or evergreen (see pages 12-15). The height, and the 'spread' for bushy herbs, can only be approximate as they depend enormously on the conditions under which the plant is grown. The 'planting distance' gives a rough idea of how far apart to place individual herbs (the 'spacing' for herbs normally sown directly in the garden), see page 30. Flowering time also depends on conditions and on when the herb was planted, and is given only when particularly relevant.

Propagation—the terms and methods used are explained in Chapter 6.

Growing conditions—the type of soil and position that the herb needs (see page 15 and Chapter 3) and whether it is suitable for growing in pots (see Chapter 13); also any special points about looking after it; otherwise follow the general instructions for maintenance given in Chapter 7.

Pests and diseases—mentioned where applicable, but most herbs are trouble-free; remedies are given on pages 50-52.

Harvesting—the parts of the plant used and the best time for the harvest; methods are given in Chapter 8.

Uses—whether the herb is used in cooking, medicine or about the house or garden.

ANGELICA
(*Angelica archangelica,* Umbelliferae)
A short-lived hardy herbaceous perennial. Height 6 feet (2m), planting distance 2 feet (60cm). Makes upright growth.

Propagation—use *fresh* seed in late summer if possible because the seeds quickly lose their viability. Sow outdoors directly in the herb garden, or sow in a pot and transfer the plants to their permanent positions in spring. Plants in the herb garden which are allowed to flower will give rise to numerous seedlings.

Growing—angelica likes a rich soil and a partially shaded position. Not suitable for growing in pots.

Harvesting—cut young tender stems for candying from May to August, and fresh green leaves for drying, if possible just before the plant flowers.

Uses—mainly used as a sweet herb for cookery.

ANISE HYSSOP

(*Agastache anethiodora*, Labiatae)
Hardy herbaceous perennial. Height 2 feet (60cm), planting distance 18 inches (45cm). Flowers July to September.

Propagation—from seed sown in pots in a greenhouse or on a windowsill in April, as it needs some warmth to germinate. Alternatively take cuttings of the soft young shoots in spring.

Growing—will grow in most ordinary soils in a sunny position. Not suitable for growing in a pot.

Harvesting—cut leaves for drying just as the flowers begin to open.

Uses—its sweet aniseed smell makes it suitable for pot-pourri; attractive purple flowers; a good bee plant.

BASIL

(*Ocimum* species, Labiatae)
Varieties—sweet basil (*Ocimum basilicum*), the usual large-leaved form reputed to have the best flavour; bush basil (*Ocimum minimum*), smaller leaves and a more compact plant; purple or 'dark opal' basil (*Ocimum basilicum purpurea*), very decorative deep purple leaves and small pink flowers. All varieties must be grown as half-hardy annuals in Britain although they are perennials in much warmer climates. Height 1–2 feet (30–60cm), planting distance 12–18 inches (30–45cm).

Propagation—from seed sown in pots indoors or in a heated propagator in March, or in a cold greenhouse in late April. Plant out around the end of May, after the last frost.

Growing—basil needs a rich well-drained soil and a warm sheltered position in the garden; prolific growth will usually only be obtained from plants in the greenhouse, although they can do well in large pots on a sunny patio.

Pests—greenfly and whitefly may be a problem with pot-grown plants.

Harvesting—pick fresh leaves during the summer and early autumn as these have by far the best flavour; keep the plant well clipped to encourage new growth; leaves can be dried with care or frozen, but are often used to make a herb oil.

Uses—a deliciously pungent culinary herb; also of some medicinal value.

BAY

(*Laurus nobilis*, Lauraceae)
Perennial; a slow-growing evergreen tree, hardy in the south once established; maximum height in Britain usually about 18 feet (6m) and natural spread 8 feet (2.4m); however trees are often clipped and/or grown in pots which restricts their growth.

Propagation—from heeled semi-ripe cuttings; these can be taken in September and overwintered in a cold frame or under a cloche, but the success rate will be low; better results may be obtained by using a heated propagator; layering shoots from an established tree is also a possibility.

Growing—in the south bay trees can be planted out in ordinary soil in a sunny sheltered position; protect young trees in cold spells during their first few winters. Where the weather is more severe, pot growing is preferable: an 18 inch (45cm) tub would take a sizeable specimen, say 6 feet (2m) tall. Clip shaped trees at least twice during the summer once established.

Pests—scale insects may infest the undersides of leaves and the stems, making the plants sticky and sooty.

Harvesting—leaves can be picked from established trees at any time and used fresh or dried.

Uses—an important culinary herb, an essential part of a *bouquet garni*; also used in some sweet dishes.

BERGAMOT

(*Monarda didyma*, Labiatae)
Varieties—nurseries may have named varieties of red bergamot (e.g. 'Cambridge Scarlet') which is the one to use for herb teas; also pink/purple varieties (like 'Croftway Pink') which are prob-

ably hybrids with wild bergamot *(Monarda fistulosa)*. All these varieties are hardy herbaceous perennials. Height 2 feet (60cm); planting distance 18 inches (45cm). Flowers June to September.

Propagation—by root division in early spring or cuttings of the first young shoots as soon as they are 3–4 inches (7.5–10cm) long; plants of ordinary red bergamot can be grown from seed sown inside in March or April, but named varieties do not come true from seed.

Growing—rich moist soil, some shade. Not suited to growing in pots.

Harvesting—pick fresh leaves during the summer; cut leaves and flowers for drying when flowers are just fully open.

Uses—an excellent herb tea; some medicinal value; attractive flowers, good for bees.

between plants but at least 2 feet (60cm) from other herbs, as they produce a lot of floppy growth.

Propagation—sow seeds in April where the plants are to grow, and again in June for a continual supply of young leaves and flowers; sporadic germination of self-sown seeds should maintain this in future years.

Growing—borage likes a sunny position, almost any soil. Not suitable for growing in pots.

Harvesting—cut the young leaves fresh throughout the summer (they do not dry well); pick flowers fresh, or for freezing or drying, when they are just fully opened.

Uses—fresh leaves give a refreshing flavour to summer salads and cold drinks; flowers used similarly for decoration, and dried to add colour to *pot-pourri*.

BORAGE
(Borago officinalis, Boraginaceae)
Self-seeding annual; height 1½–2½ feet (45–75cm); spacing 1 foot (30cm)

CARAWAY
(Carum carvi, Umbelliferae)
Hardy biennial. Height 18 inches (45cm); planting distance 9 inches

Rosemary and creeping thymes do well on top of low walls.

A wooden seat hidden at the end of a path in the herb garden, surrounded by flowering scented herbs.

Borage flowers are always popular with bees.

D. Goodall

Red bergamot flowers make a colourful show and a delicious herb tea.

Lawn chamomile forms a close mat between 'stepping' stones.

(23cm). Makes upright growth.

Propagation—sow seed in May/June where the plants are to grow, or sow in pots outdoors and transplant in early autumn.

Growing—best harvests are obtained from plants growing in fertile, well-drained soil in full sun. Not suitable for growing in pots.

Harvesting—collect the seeds in late summer the following year.

Uses—seeds traditionally used in cakes and bread, and in some pickles and cheeses.

CHAMOMILE
(Compositae)

Species and named varieties—'common' or 'Roman' chamomile *(Anthemis nobilis)* is a perennial with single white daisy flowers (used for herb tea) and creeping, sweetly scented foliage. Although this will make a 'lawn' if it is kept clipped, the variety 'Treneague' which is very low growing and does not flower is preferable; there is also an attractive 'double-flowered' variety. German chamomile *(Matricaria chamomilla)* is a self-seeding annual, similar to common Roman chamomile in appearance, but not suitable for lawns. *Anthemis nobilis* varieties stay green in winter. Heights 1 foot (30cm) for double and unclipped Roman chamomile, 2 inches (6cm) for the Treneague variety; 18 inches (45cm) for German chamomile; space plants about 6 inches (15cm) apart when used for ground cover otherwise allow 18 inches (45cm).

Propagation—perennial varieties from 'offsets' or clusters of young shoots, best taken in late spring or early autumn; they root easily in trays in a cold greenhouse, frame or even outside in a semi-shaded position. The common variety can also be grown from seed sown outdoors in late spring, which is useful for large numbers of ground cover plants; unless the area is small and very weed free, it is preferable to sow in trays and transplant. Sow German chamomile directly in the garden in spring or early summer. The seed is very fine.

Growing—chamomile will grow in almost any soil, in a fairly sunny position; 'lawn' areas must be kept well weeded at first; gaps often appear in the centre of established areas and should be filled with offsets from the outside, set in a little fresh soil, in spring. Single plants of common or double chamomile can be grown in troughs or pots.

Harvesting—cut flowers for drying when they are just fully out (mid-summer).

Uses—as a herb tea which is soothing and an aid to digestion.

CHERVIL

(*Anthriscus cerefolium,* Umbelliferae)
Self-seeding hardy annual. Height 1–2
feet (30–60cm), spacing 9–12 inches
(23–30cm).

Propagation—from fresh seed sown
directly in its growing position during
spring or late summer. Plants sown in
midsummer tend to bolt quickly.

Growing—chervil will grow on most
soils, but moisture and partial shade are
necessary for summer grown plants.
Cloche autumn sown plants for winter
use. Not suitable for pot growing
except in winter in a cold greenhouse.

Harvesting—cut fresh leaves all year
round. Does not dry well but will
freeze.

Uses—a useful delicately flavoured
culinary herb.

allow seedlings to grow up to form a
clump; established clumps can be divided to increase stock.

Growing—chives produce best
growth in a rich moist soil in a fairly
sunny position. Every few years clumps
should be lifted, divided and replanted
into soil that has had compost or
manure freshly added. Grows well in
pots if regularly fed.

Pests—greenfly may be a problem on
pot-grown plants.

Harvesting—cut clumps across to
within an inch or two of the ground to
provide leaves for use fresh or for
freezing; does not dry well.

Uses—a popular culinary herb for its
mild onion flavour, mainly added to
salads or as a garnish after cooking.
Attractive edging plant if some clumps
are allowed to flower.

CHIVES

(*Allium schoenaprasum,* Liliaceae)
Perennial. Dies down in winter. Height
8 inches (20cm), grows in clumps,
planting distance from other herbs 1
foot (30cm).

Propagation—from seed sown thinly
in the garden or in a pot in March;

COMFREY

(*Symphytum* species, Boraginaceae)
Species—wild or common comfrey
(*Symphytum officinale*) has white, pink
or purple flowers; Russian comfrey
(*Symphytum uplandicum*) has blue/pur-
ple flowers and is more vigorous. Both

species are hardy, herbaceous perennials. Height and spread 3 feet (1m); growth is floppy but plants grown for liquid fertilizer will be constantly clipped; nevertheless they are deep-rooted and difficult to get rid of.

Propagation—grows easily from root cuttings or offsets, or by division.

Growing—comfrey likes a damp position and needs a rich soil for maximum leaf growth. Not suitable for growing in pots.

Diseases—sometimes suffers from rust.

Harvesting—cut plants across with shears to provide foliage for making liquid feed, from early summer to autumn (they will give four cuttings if well fed). For medicinal use leaves can be cut fresh, dried or frozen; dig roots in autumn for drying.

Uses—a valuable healing herb for all kinds of cuts, aches and pains; useful in the garden for plant feeding and compost making.

CORIANDER

(*Coriandrum sativum*, Umbelliferae)
Hardy annual. Height 12–18 inches (30–45cm), space plants for seed 6

inches (15cm) apart and 18 inches (45cm) from other herbs; makes upright growth on a fine stem.

Propagation—from seed sown in its growing position; sow in May or June, and thin out if plants are being grown for their seed; successive sowings can be made for closely spaced leaf crops.

Growing—coriander needs a light soil and a sunny, sheltered position. Not very suitable for growing in pots.

Harvesting—cut broad young seedling leaves for fresh use; they do not dry well. Collect seeds when they have turned from green to brown.

Uses—young leaves used mostly in Indian cooking; seeds in spicy, savoury and sweet dishes.

COSTMARY

(*Balsamita vulgaris*, Compositae)
Sometimes called 'alecost'. Hardy herbaceous perennial. Height 2 feet 6 inches (75cm), planting distance 2 feet (60cm).

Propagation—by division or offsets.

Growing—costmary will grow in

most soils but likes a sunny position. Not suitable for growing in pots.

Harvesting—cut leaves for drying, preferably just before flowering.

Uses—their sweet balsam-like scent makes the leaves a good addition to pot-pourri; culinary and medicinal uses are sometimes recommended.

COTTON LAVENDER

(*Santolina chamaecyparissus*, Compositae)
Varieties—there are several similar species and named varieties available (including green and dwarf forms) but the silver-grey *S. chamaecyparissus* is the commonest. It is a shrubby, evergreen perennial. Height and spread can be up to 2 feet (60cm) but it is best kept clipped. Spacing for hedge plants 15–18 inches (37–45cm).

Propagation—from soft or semi-ripe stem cuttings taken in spring or early autumn; it roots easily.

Growing—these shrubs grow best on a well-drained soil in full sun. They should be cut hard after flowering or in the early spring or the bushes will open up and loose their attractive shape. Hedges will need regular clipping. Not

suitable for growing in pots.

Harvesting—cut leaves for drying at any time during the summer.

Uses—leaves used as a moth repellent; an attractive border plant.

CURRY PLANT

(*Helichrysum angustifolium*, Compositae)
A shrubby evergreen perennial with silver foliage. Height and spread 18 inches (45cm); planting distance for hedge 1 foot (30cm).

Propagation—from soft or semi-ripe stem cuttings taken in spring or early autumn, it roots fairly easily.

Growing—curry plants thrive in any well-drained soil in a sunny position; not very good for growing in pots.

Harvesting—flowers for drying when they are fully open; fresh leaves in spring, summer and autumn.

Uses—curry plants make an attractive addition to the garden with some curiosity value as they give off a strong smell of curry even if untouched; surprisingly, the leaves only carry a very mild flavour and are seldom used in the kitchen. The bright yellow button flowers add colour to pot-pourri.

DILL

(*Anethum graveolens*, Umbelliferae)
Hardy annual, sometimes self-seeding. Height 2 feet 6 inches (75cm), spacing for seed plants 9–12 inches (23–30cm).

Propagation—sow seed where the crop is to grow; for a seed crop start in April; for a supply of young leaves make successive sowings up to midsummer.

Growing—dill likes a well-drained soil and a sunny sheltered position; may need staking. Not suitable for growing in pots.

Harvesting—cut fresh leaves before flowering, and fresh unopen flowerheads for adding to pickles; these do not dry well but will freeze. Collect seeds as they begin to turn brown.

Uses—an important culinary herb, traditional in Scandinavian cooking; also used medicinally for its digestive properties.

en and variegated varieties are available. All varieties are hardy deciduous shrubs or small trees; height and spread 12 feet (4m) but can be restricted. Grows vigorously. Flowers in June.

Propagation—from semi-ripe heeled cuttings taken in late summer. The wild elder readily self-seeds.

Growing—elder will grow in any soil; needs a sunny or partially shaded position. Not suitable for growing in pots. Prune to keep in shape between October and March.

Pests—blackfly may infest young stems and leaves in spring, although these will not hurt a large tree.

Harvesting—pick flowerheads for using fresh and for drying in June when they are fully open; berries for using fresh or freezing when they turn black in autumn.

Uses—flowers used in sweet dishes and drinks; berries in fruit pies and jellies; the flowers, berries and leaves have important medicinal uses.

ELDER
(*Sambucus nigra,* Caprifoliacae)
Varieties—common, wild elder, found in hedgerows is best for culinary and medicinal use; various ornamental gold-

FENNEL
(*Foeniculum vulgare,* Umbelliferae)
Varieties—common fennel with green feathery foliage; 'bronze' fennel, similar with a striking reddish tint. ('Florence'

fennel is grown as a vegetable and is not considered here.) Common and bronze fennel are hardy perennials, dying down in winter. Height 5 feet (1.5m), planting distance 2 feet (60cm). Strong, stiff upright growth.

Propagation—by dividing clumps, or from seed sown outdoors in the ground or in a pot in spring. Germinates easily.

Growing—fennel does best in well-drained but fairly rich soil in a sunny position. Keep some shoots cut to confine the plant and provide fresh young leaves. Can be grown in a pot if fed and clipped regularly.

Harvesting—cut fresh leaves during summer and early autumn (they do not dry well but will freeze); stalks for drying as available; seeds in autumn.

Uses—a common culinary herb with aniseed flavour, traditionally used with fish; used medicinally for its digestive properties.

here. It is a short-lived hardy herbaceous perennial. Height 2 feet (60cm), spread 18 inches (45cm).

Propagation—from seed sown any time from March to August. It germinates readily and will self-seed in future years.

Growing—feverfew will grow in any soil in a sunny position; it could be grown in pots to supply leaves if kept clipped. Replace old plants with self-sown seedlings every two or three years.

Harvesting—cut leaves throughout the growing season for using fresh or drying.

Uses—a traditional medicinal herb, which has recently gained a reputation for helping migraine.

FEVERFEW
(*Chrysanthemum parthenium*, Compositae)
Varieties—there are various cultivated forms but it is the single-flowered common feverfew that is described

GARLIC
(*Allium sativum*, Liliaceae)
Grown as a hardy annual from bulblets. Height 18 inches (45cm), planting distance 6 inches (15cm). Each bulblet produces a few thin flat upright leaves.

Propagation—split garlic bulbs into individual bulblets or 'cloves' and plant these in October, November or early March, 2 inches (5cm) deep.

Growing—garlic does best on a light but well-manured soil in a sunny position. Keep well weeded. Not suitable for growing in pots.

Diseases—can be affected by white rot which causes yellowing of the foliage and white fungal growth on the bulbs. Remove infected plants and avoid using this ground for garlic again.

Harvesting—lift bulbs when the leaves die down in July or August and dry thoroughly in a warm airy place.

Uses—garlic is a very pungent but indispensable culinary herb; it is also very important medicinally for its antiseptic and other properties.

Heights and spreads vary from 9 inches–2 feet (23–60cm), but they can be kept cut back.

Propagation—from cuttings of soft shoots taken in early spring or August; they root easier if in some heat.

Growing—scented geraniums can be bedded out in the garden after the last frost in an open sunny position; however, they do very well if kept in pots stood out during the summer and kept indoors or in a frost-free greenhouse in winter.

Pests and diseases—white fly, grey mould and root-rot may affect plants indoors but should not be a problem during the summer.

Harvesting—pick leaves for use fresh or for drying during the growing season.

Uses—mainly in pot-pourri, but lemon and rose-scented varieties are sometimes used in cooking.

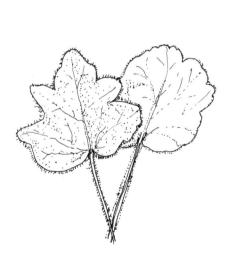

GERANIUMS, SCENTED
(*Pelargonium* species, Geraniaceae)
Species and named varieties—there are many, with scents variously described as 'lemon', 'pine', 'cedar', 'rose' and 'orange'. The lemon scented *Pelargonium graveolens* is one of the most common and most useful. All are half-hardy evergreen perennials.

HEARTSEASE
(*Viola tricolor*, Violaceae)
Varieties—the common heartsease used by herbalists has tiny purple/yellow

pansy flowers, although there are other forms available. They are hardy perennials. Height and spacing 6 inches (15cm). Heartsease will flower throughout the growing season.

Propagation—from seed sown in the garden or in pots in spring or late summer. It germinates easily and many self-sown seedlings will be produced.

Growing—heartsease will grow in any soil, in sun or partial shade. Clip back growth to young basal shoots after flowering. Can be grown in pots.

Harvesting—flowers and leaves for use fresh and for drying can be picked from spring right through until late autumn.

Uses—the flowers will decorate sweet dishes and salads; the whole plant is used medicinally.

Propagation—best from cuttings of young shoots in early spring; seed needs cold treatment, may be difficult to germinate, and will also give some unwanted male plants.

Growing—hops need a deep rich soil and a sunny position; cut back the plants hard in the autumn after harvesting.

Harvesting—the young shoots can be eaten fresh in salad but hops are mainly grown for their cone-like female flowers which are cut for drying in the early autumn.

Uses—the dried flowers are used in beer-making, herb teas and herb pillows. An important medicinal herb, known for its sedative properties.

HOPS

(*Humulus lupulus,* Cannabinaceae)
Varieties—there are both green and gold-leaved forms. A hardy perennial climber. Height 18 feet (6m). Male and female flowers usually occur on separate plants.

HORSERADISH

(*Cochlearia armoracia,* Cruciferae)
A hardy herbaceous perennial. Height 2 feet (60cm); planting distance from other herbs 2 feet (60cm). A vigorous grower, tenacious and invasive.

Propagation—from root cuttings about 6 inches (15cm) long spaced 12 inches (30cm) apart, planted vertically so that their tops are 2 inches (5cm) below ground. Start them off in February to harvest roots in autumn.

Growing—horseradish will grow almost anywhere, but deep, light, well-manured soil, in sun or partial shade, will give the best roots. If a large quantity is required, horseradish should be given a patch of its own where the roots can be lifted and the soil replenished each autumn.

Pests and diseases—cabbage white caterpillars may feed on leaves during late summer; the leaves may also be affected by some fungus diseases but these should not be a problem on vigorous well-grown plants.

Harvesting—dig the fresh roots for use at any time from established plants only, and in the autumn for drying or making an extract in alcohol. Roots can also be stored in boxes of damp sand in a cool place.

Uses—in cooking to make a pungent sauce; also many medicinal uses.

white flowered forms. A hardy perennial shrub, evergreen in mild winters. Height 18 inches (45cm), spread 2 feet (60cm); planting distance for a hedge 1 foot (30cm). Flowers July to September.

Propagation—from seed sown in pots indoors in March or from cuttings of young shoots in late spring.

Growing—hyssop will grow in most well-drained soils in a sunny position. Cut bushes and flowering hedges into shape in late August after flowering; keep formal hedges well-clipped during the growing season.

Harvesting—cut young leaves for drying in summer.

Uses—hyssop's pungent, rather bitter smell makes it suitable for some pot-pourris, particularly moth repellent mixtures; it is an excellent bee and butterfly plant; it is also of some medicinal value.

HYSSOP

(*Hyssopus officinalis*, Labiatae)
Varieties—the common hyssop has blue flowers but there are also pink and

LADY'S MANTLE

(*Alchemilla mollis*, Rosaceae)
A hardy, herbaceous perennial. Height 1 foot (30cm), spread 18 inches (45cm). Forms an attractively shaped

mound. Flowers June to August.

Propagation—from seeds sown in pots or in the garden in March; they germinate readily and established plants produce many self-sown seedlings; such plants can also be divided in autumn or early spring.

Growing—lady's mantle is a tolerant plant, growing in any soil, in sun or partial shade. Clip off all old growth in September. Could be grown in troughs.

Harvesting—cut young leaves for use throughout the summer and harvest for drying as the plant comes into flower.

Uses—a traditional medicinal herb for 'women's complaints'; an attractive border plant; excellent for flower arrangement.

Propagation—from semi-ripe cuttings taken in August. Some varieties can be grown from seed: sow in pots in spring with some heat if possible; germination may be slow and variable, and the quality of the plants unpredictable.

Growing—lavender will grow in any well-drained soil in a sunny position. Cut off dead flowerheads and trim bushes in late summer.

Pests—leaf-hoppers (which produce cuckoo spit) are often in evidence, but should not harm established plants.

Harvesting—cut flowers for drying when they are about half open.

Uses—dried flowers famous for use in pot-pourri and scented sachets; an attractive border plant, very popular with bees and butterflies.

LAVENDER
(*Lavandula* species, Labiatae)
Species and named varieties—the most commonly available are varieties of *Lavandula spica* and *Lavandula vera*, some of which are described in Table 5. They are hardy evergreen shrubs, heights and (almost equal) spreads ranging from 1–3 feet (30cm–1m). Hedging plants should be spaced 9–12 inches (23–30cm) apart. They flower from July to September.

LEMON BALM
(*Melissa officinalis,* Labiatae)
Varieties—there are golden and variegated varieties as well as the common green form. All are hardy herbaceous perennials. Height 2–3 feet (60cm–1m), planting distance 18 inches (45cm).

Propagation—from cuttings of young shoots in early spring or by division of clumps; the common form can also be grown from seed sown in the garden or in pots in May; it germinates readily and self-sown seedlings are produced from established plants.

Growing—lemon balm makes best growth in fairly rich moist soil in a sunny position, although it is a tolerant plant. Keep all plants trimmed round the edge to restrict growth and give fresh shoots. Variegated forms may need cutting back completely in June for continual colourful foliage.

Diseases—variegated forms may get rusty patches on leaves later in the summer: cut back foliage as described above.

Harvesting—cut fresh leaves throughout the summer and for drying just before flowering begins.

Uses—lemon balm makes a pleasant herb tea with some medicinal properties; its cream flowers are indistinctive but nevertheless very popular with bees.

Propagation—by 3 inch (7.5cm) cuttings of young lateral shoots in early summer. Root in a pot with some heat.

Growing—in very mild south-western areas lemon verbena can be planted out in a sunny sheltered position. Otherwise it should be planted in a greenhouse border or grown in a large pot—a 1 foot (30cm) one will accommodate a usefully sized shrub. Pots must be kept frost free in a greenhouse or conservatory during the winter. The shrubs tend to straggle and should be pruned into shape in March before growth begins. They are slow to come into leaf.

Pests—whitefly can be a problem on greenhouse plants.

Harvesting—pick leaves for use fresh during the summer and early autumn, and for drying just before the shrub flowers.

Uses—the sweet lemon-scented leaves make a delicious herb tea, and are a useful addition to pot-pourri.

LEMON VERBENA
(*Lippia citriodora*, Verbenaceae)
A deciduous half-hardy perennial shrub. Height 5 feet (1.5m), spread 4 feet (1.2m), but is usually restricted by growing in a pot.

LOVAGE
(*Levisticum officinalis*, Umbelliferae)
A hardy herbaceous perennial. Height 6 feet (2m), planting distance 2 feet

(60cm). Produces strong upright growth, but can be kept clipped.

Propagation—by division of established clumps or from seed sown in the spring in the garden or in pots.

Growing—lovage grows best on a fairly rich moist soil, in sun or partial shade. Cut round the edges of clumps to restrict spread and produce young shoots. Staking may be necessary. Can be grown in a pot if fed well and kept clipped.

Pests—sometimes suffers from leaf miner.

Harvesting—cut young leaves for use fresh throughout summer and for drying before the plant flowers; collect seeds when they ripen in September.

Uses—its strong yeasty taste makes lovage a useful culinary herb.

MARIGOLD, POT

(*Calendula officinalis,* Compositae)
A hardy self-seeding annual. Height 18 inches (45cm); spacing 12 inches (30cm). Flowers May to October.

Propagation—from seed sown in the garden in spring or late summer; germinates readily.

Growing—marigolds are very tolerant plants, and will thrive in any soil in a sunny position. They can be grown in pots, but tend to straggle; autumn sown ones kept in a greenhouse will flower very early.

Pests and diseases—slugs can be a particular problem; leaves sometimes become covered with powdery mildew.

Harvesting—pick flowers for use fresh and for drying throughout the summer.

Uses—bright yellow flowers, attractive in the garden, used to add colour to salads and some cooked dishes, and also to pot-pourri. A traditional and effective healing herb.

MARJORAM

(*Origanum* species, Labiatae)
Species and varieties—wild marjoram or 'oregano' *(Origanum vulgare)* and pot marjoram *(Origanum onites)* are hardy, semi-shrubby perennials; height and spread 15 inches (38cm); they are often hard to distinguish; although 'oregano' has a very pungent flavour when grown in its native Mediterranean conditions, it becomes very similar to pot marjoram when grown in the garden; it has an attractive golden form. Sweet or 'knotted' marjoram *(Origanum majorana)* is usually grown as a half-hardy annual, although it is a perennial in warmer climates and can be overwinterd in pots indoors; height and spread is 1 foot (30cm); it has small 'knots' of white flowers and a strong but sweet distinctive flavour.

Propagation—wild and pot marjoram can be grown from seed sown in the garden or in pots in April; also by division of established plants or from cuttings of young basal shoots taken in spring or late summer. Sweet marjoram is grown from seed sown in pots in March or April in some heat.

Growing—all the marjorams like a light well-drained soil and a sunny position; sweet marjoram should not be planted out until the end of May. All do well grown in pots.

Harvesting—wild and pot marjoram do not dry well but shoots can be picked fresh from spring to late autumn; sweet marjoram can be dried very successfully from shoots containing leaves and flowers throughout the summer.

Uses—all marjorams are useful culinary herbs: mild pot marjoram for salads or as a last minute addition to savoury dishes; dried sweet marjoram in spicy winter cookery.

MEADOWSWEET

(*Filipendula ulmaria*, Rosaceae)
A hardy perennial. Height 3 feet (1m), planting distance 18 inches (45cm). Flowers July, August. Stiff upright growth.

Propagation—by division of clumps or from seed sown in the garden in late

spring or early autumn.

Growing—meadowsweet is a native of damp, marshy places; sun or partial shade. Not suitable for growing in pots.

Harvesting—leaves for drying in midsummer; flowers for drying when just fully open.

Uses—a very useful and versatile medicinal herb; its white frothy flowers make it a pleasing garden plant.

MINT

(*Mentha* species, Labiatae)
Species and named varieties—applemint (*Mentha rotundifolia*) height 3 feet (1m); Corsican mint (*Mentha requienii*) very low ground cover; eau-de-Cologne mint (*Mentha citrata*) height 18 inches (45cm); ginger mint (*Mentha gentilis*) height 1 foot (30cm), green/gold variegated leaves; peppermint (*Mentha piperita*) height 18 inches (45cm); pineapple mint (*Mentha rotundifolia*, variegated) height 15 inches (38cm), cream/green leaves, floppy growth; spearmint (*Mentha viridis*) height 18

MULLEIN
(*Verbascum thapsus*, Scrophulariaceae)
A hardy self-seeding biennial. Height 3 feet (1m), spacing 1 foot (30cm). Flowers on a single upright spike from June to August.

Propagation—from seed sown in the garden or in pots in April; germinates readily; not suitable for growing in pots.

Growing—mullein will grow in any well-drained soil in a sunny position.

Pests—mullein moth caterpillar feeds on leaves.

Harvesting—flowers for use fresh, or for drying (or preferably freezing) as soon as they appear; leaves for drying in early summer.

inches (45cm), the common garden mint.

Propagation—Corsican mint by division in March or April; all other varieties by root division or root cuttings, or from cuttings of young shoots in early spring.

Growing—mints will grow in any soil, but a rich moist soil and partially shaded position is preferable. All varieties except Corsican mint are invasive, but roots can be restricted (see page 35) and plants should be clipped round the outside when necessary. Can be grown in pots if fed and clipped, and frequently renewed.

Diseases—mint rust may effect leaves and stems, especially of spearmint; applemint is fairly resistant to rust but may be affected by powdery mildew.

Harvesting—cut leaves for use fresh throughout the summer; harvest for drying when flowers are half open.

Uses—applemint and spearmint are common culinary herbs; peppermint is a powerful medicinal herb, most used for its effect on the digestive system; pineapple, ginger and eau-de-Cologne mints are sweet herbs for pot-pourri, and attractive foliage plants.

Uses—a medicinal herb, traditional for respiratory complaints; a striking garden plant.

NASTURTIUM
(*Tropaeolum majus*, Tropaeolaceae)
Varieties—the vigorous trailing or climbing nasturtiums will cover 6 feet (2m) or more; semi-trailing (or 'Gleam') varieties, height and spacing 15 inches (38cm), grow bushy and

tinge in May.

Propagation—by division of rhizomes after flowering or in early autumn.

Growing—these irises like a good, well-drained soil and a sunny position; trim leaves in winter; clumps should be divided and replanted about every three years. Not suitable for growing in pots.

make shorter runners; dwarf ('Tom Thumb') varieties, height and spacing 10 inches (25cm), stay compact. All are hardy self-seeding annuals, with bright orange/red flowers from June to September.

Propagation—from seed sown in the garden or in pots in April; germinates readily.

Growing—nasturtiums are very tolerant; most flowers are produced on *poor* soil in a sunny position. Will grow in troughs and pots.

Pests—leaves and stems may become infested with blackfly.

Harvesting—fresh leaves and flowers throughout the summer; seed pods when green; often put into vinegar.

Uses—the peppery flavoured leaves are good in salads and the flowers are used to decorate them; green seed pods can be used as caper substitutes.

ORRIS

(*Iris florentina*, Iridaceae)
A hardy perennial. Height 2–3 feet (60cm–1m), planting distance 15 inches (38cm). White flowers with purple

Harvesting—lift rhizomes for drying in autumn.

Uses—the dried rhizomes are powdered or grated as a fixative in pot-pourri. An attractive garden plant.

PARSLEY

(*Petroselinum crispum*, Umbelliferae)
Varieties—the crispy 'curled' varieties are most commonly grown; there is also a plain-leaved 'French' parsley; ('Hamburg' parsley is grown as a vegetable for its edible root and is not considered here). These varieties are hardy biennials. Height 1 foot (30cm), spacing 9 inches (23cm).

Propagation—from seed sown in the garden in May or late summer, or in early spring in pots with some heat; seed is very slow to germinate, and this

for growing in pots.

Harvesting—young fresh leaves throughout the growing season; can be cut as a seedling crop.

Uses—spicy leaves added to salad.

accounts for most failures—heat is the best remedy.

Growing—parsley needs a rich, moist soil and a partially shaded summer position; it can be picked throughout a mild winter if cloched. It will grow successfully in pots if fed well.

Pests—carrot fly maggots sometimes attack the roots and can cause young plants to wilt and die.

Harvesting—pick leaves for use fresh nearly all year and for freezing in summer; parsley does not dry well.

Uses—a common but indispensable culinary herb; also has valuable medicinal properties.

ROCKET

(*Eruca sativa*, Cruciferae)
Self-seeding hardy annual. Height 2 feet (60cm), spacing 6 inches (15cm).

Propagation—sow in the garden in March, April or late summer: it bolts quickly in midsummer; germination is quick and easy.

Growing—rocket will grow in most soils; in summer it does best in partial shade; autumn sowings can be cloched for use in very early spring. Not suitable

ROSEMARY

(*Rosmarinus officinalis*, Labiatae)
Varieties—named varieties are often distinguished by their flower colour (from very pale grey blue to dark blue) and sometimes by their nature of growth (from spiky and upright to low and drooping). 'Mrs Jessups Upright' has pale blue flowers, erect growth and is probably the hardiest variety; 'Severn Sea' has dark blue flowers, arching branches, and is much less hardy. All are evergreen shrubs, hardy in sheltered positions in the south. Height varies from 1 foot (30cm) for spreading varieties to a more usual 2–3 feet (60cm–1m) for upright varieties, spread 3 feet (1m). Spacing for hedging plants 18 inches (45cm). Flowers March and April.

Propagation—from cuttings of young shoots taken in early spring, semi-ripe cuttings taken after flowering, or by layering. Common rosemary can also be grown from seed sown in late spring with some heat, but germination may be difficult and named varieties do not come true from seed.

Growing—rosemary needs a light well-drained soil and a sunny sheltered position, with some protection given to young plants in severe weather. Any trimming necessary is best carried out in late spring after flowering. Rosemary does well in pots and this is a good way to grow it in cold districts. Bushes are best replaced about every six years.

Harvesting—pick sprigs for use fresh at any time during the growing season, and for drying preferably as the bush comes into flower.

Uses—a pleasantly pungent culinary herb, for sweet as well as savoury dishes; also has useful medicinal properties. An attractive garden shrub.

Salvia rutilans, and is not considered here. All the green and purple sages are hardy evergreen shrubs, although the 'Tricolor' variety cannot stand cold, wet conditions. Height 20 inches (50cm), spread 2 feet (60cm).

Propagation—from heeled cuttings of young shoots in late spring or early autumn, or by layering. The common green sage can also be grown from seed sown in pots in April.

Growing—sage grows best in a light, well-drained soil and a sunny position; also grows well in pots. Trim new growth hard after flowering. Bushes should be replaced every three or four years.

Harvesting—pick leaves for use fresh at any time, and for drying preferably just before the bushes flower.

Uses—a traditional culinary herb with a strong flavour; also much used medicinally, particularly for its digestive and antiseptic properties; the coloured forms are very attractive garden plants.

SAGE
(*Salvia officinalis,* Labiatae)
Varieties—common green sage has narrow leaves and purple flowers; a similar broad-leaved form rarely flowers; there is also a purple-leaved 'red' sage ('Purpurascens') and two variegated forms: green/gold ('Icterina') and cream/grey/purple ('Tricolor'). The half-hardy 'pineapple sage' is a different species,

SALAD BURNET
(*Sanguisorba minor,* Rosaceae)
A hardy perennial, keeping green

foliage throughout the winter. Height and spread 1 foot (30cm). Compact growth.

Propagation—from seed sown in the garden or in pots in March and April or in late summer; it germinates readily and established plants sometimes self-seed.

Growing—salad burnet is a native of chalk downlands, and thus likes a limy, well-drained soil, sun or partial shade. Will grow well in pots.

Harvesting—leaves for use fresh all the year round. It does not dry well, but is often put into a herb vinegar.

Uses—leaves useful in salads and as a garnish, particularly in winter.

Growing—summer savory grows best in a moderately fertile, well-drained soil, in a sunny position. Can be grown in pots.

Harvesting—pick shoots for use fresh from midsummer until September, and for drying as the plant comes into flower. Summer savory dries well.

Uses—a good culinary herb of distinctive flavour, traditionally used in bean dishes.

SAVORY, WINTER
(*Satureia montana*, Labiatae)
Varieties—the common form has white flowers and there is also a smaller purple flowered variety '*coerulea*'. A hardy shrub, evergreen in mild winters. Height 6–12 inches (15–30cm), spread 12–18 inches (30–45cm), spacing for hedging plants (common variety) 1 foot (30cm).

Propagation—from seed sown in pots in April, or from cuttings of young shoots in late spring.

Growing—winter savory needs a light well-drained soil and a sunny position. Little trimming is necessary except for hedges. Grows well in pots.

SAVORY, SUMMER
(*Satureia hortensis*, Labiatae)
Annual. Height 1 foot (30cm), spacing 6–9 inches (15–23cm). Stiff bushy growth.

Propagation—from seed sown in the garden or, preferably, in pots in April.

Harvesting—pick shoots for use fresh throughout the growing season and for drying as the bush comes into flower.

Uses—as for summer savory; winter savory can also be used medicinally.

SORREL

(Rumex species, Polygonaceae)
Species and named varieties—common or garden sorrel *(Rumex acetosa)* has broad leaves, upright growth, height 2 feet 6 inches (75cm); buckler-leaved sorrel *(Rumex scutatus)* has small leaves, spreading growth, height 18 inches (45cm). The name 'French sorrel' is sometimes given to *R. scutatus* and sometimes to a narrow-leaved form of *R. acetosa*. All the sorrels are hardy herbaceous perennials. Planting distance 1 foot (30cm).

Propagation—from seed sown in the garden or in pots in late March or April; also by division of clumps in autumn or early spring.

Growing—sorrel produces best growth in a moderately rich moist soil, in sun or partial shade; it can be grown in pots if clipped and well fed but

comparatively little foliage is produced. The tall flower spikes of garden sorrel should be removed to encourage leafy growth.

Pests—slugs and occasionally leaf miners may attack sorrel, but should cause no problems with vigorous plants.

Harvesting—pick young leaves for use fresh and for freezing throughout the growing season; sorrel does not dry well.

Uses—the sharp tasting leaves are useful in salads, soups and sauces; sorrel also has some medicinal properties.

SOUTHERNWOOD

(Artemisia abrotanum, Compositae)
A hardy perennial shrub which keeps its leaves in mild winters. Height and spread 3 feet (1m).

Propagation—from cuttings of young shoots in spring or semi-ripe cuttings in late summer.

Growing—southernwood will grow in any ordinary well-drained soil in a sunny position. Trim the bush hard in early spring to keep it in shape. Not suitable for growing in pots.

Harvesting—pick shoots for drying in midsummer.

Uses—the pungent smell of the foliage is reputed to repel insects; an attractive garden shrub.

SWEET CICELY
(*Myrrhis odorata*, Umbelliferae)
A hardy herbaceous perennial. Height and planting distance 2 feet (60cm).

Propagation—sow fresh seed in the garden in autumn for best results; although sweet cicely self-seeds readily, packeted seed can be difficult to germinate; if sowing in spring, try giving it a 'cold spell' in the refrigerator first. Clumps of the plant can be divided in autumn or early spring.

Growing—sweet cicely is a native of damp places and grows best in moist soil and partial shade. Not suitable for growing in pots.

Harvesting—cut young leaves and stems as required, from early spring to September; they do not dry well.

Uses—a sweet culinary herb traditionally stewed with tart fruits. Sometimes used medicinally.

TARRAGON
(*Artemisia dracunculus*, Compositae)
Varieties—French tarragon, height and

planting distance 20 inches (50cm), has a clean, sharp taste and is the recommended culinary tarragon; Russian tarragon, height 3 feet (1m), planting distance 2 feet (60cm) is more vigorous but has a different, slightly bitter flavour. Both varieties are hardy, herbaceous perennials although French tarragon is more delicate until well established.

Propagation—by division, or by cuttings of young shoots from the base of the clump in early spring; Russian tarragon can also be grown from seed.

Growing—tarragon needs a light, well-drained soil and a sunny position. Protect young plants of French tarragon in winter, and divide and replant clumps every three or four years. This variety also grows well in pots.

Harvesting—pick leaves for using fresh throughout the growing season and for freezing, preferably in the midsummer months; tarragon does not dry well but makes a good herb vinegar.

Uses—an important culinary herb generally used in mild-flavoured egg and poultry dishes, added near the end of cooking.

THYME
(*Thymus* species, Labiatae)

Species and named varieties—there are many varieties of both bushy and creeping thymes. The most useful upright varieties are the common garden thyme *(Thymus vulgaris)* and lemon thyme *(Thymus × citriodorus)*; both these have gold, variegated and silver forms (see Table 13). The wild creeping thyme *(Thymus serpyllum)* with pink flowers is a neat and fast creeper and can be grown from seed; varieties of it are also easily obtainable: *'albus'* with white flowers, *'coccineus'* with rich crimson flowers and *'lanuginosum'* with grey woolly leaves. Caraway thyme *(Thymus herba-barona)* has its own subtle flavour. All varieties are hardy evergreen perennials, although some of the lemon and variegated forms need more care than common thyme. Upright varieties, height 6–9 inches (15–23cm), planting distance 1 foot (30cm); creeping varieties, height 1–3 inches (2.5–7.5cm), planting distance to form ground cover 6–9 inches (15–23cm).

Propagation—upright varieties, from soft-shoot cuttings in late spring or by layering; common thyme can also be grown easily from seed sown in pots in early spring; creeping varieties are increased by division in spring or early autumn.

Growing—thymes need a well-drained, preferably limy soil and full sun. Trim upright varieties hard after flowering to encourage bushy growth; the plants may need replacing every three or four years. Cloche less hardy forms in severe or very wet and cold weather if possible. All varieties grow well in pots.

Harvesting—cut shoots of garden and lemon thymes for using fresh throughout the growing season and for drying just before the plants flower; they dry well.

Uses—garden thyme is a major culinary herb, traditionally included in *bouquet garni*, and is also important medicinally, particularly for its antiseptic properties; lemon thyme is used in sweet dishes and as a tea. The coloured forms make very decorative, compact garden plants.

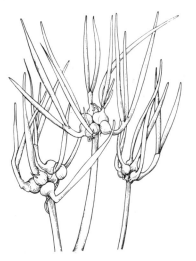

TREE ONION
(*Allium cepa proliferum*, Alliaceae)

Hardy perennial. Height 3 feet (1m), planting distance from other herbs 18 inches (45cm). Upright growth, producing small onion 'bulbils' in clusters on the tips of the leaves.

Propagation—plant single bulbils or clusters 9 inches (23cm) apart in spring or autumn.

Growing—tree onions prefer a fertile well-drained soil and a sunny position; renew or thin out clumps every few years.

Harvesting—pick onion clusters as available, often throughout the winter.

Uses—provides fresh onion flavour for cooking throughout the year; bulbils can also be pickled.

WORMWOOD
(*Artemisia absinthium*, Compositae)
A hardy perennial. Height 3 feet (1m), planting distance 2–3 feet (60cm–1m). Semi-shrubby growth.

Propagation—from cuttings of young shoots in spring or semi-ripe cuttings in late summer; or from seed sown in pots indoors in late spring, germination can be erratic.

Growing—wormwood will grow in any ordinary soil in a sunny position; cut back growth to within 6 inches (15cm) of the ground in autumn or early spring. Not suitable for growing in pots.

Harvesting—cut leaves for drying in midsummer.

Uses—its pungent bitter smell is reputed to repel insects.

YARROW
(*Achillea millefolium*, Compositae)
Varieties—the native yarrow used by herbalists has white or slightly pinkish flowers, but there are garden varieties with bright yellow or red flowers. All varieties are hardy herbaceous perennials. Height 20 inches (50cm), planting distance 15 inches (38cm). Flowers June to September.

Propagation—by division of clumps in early spring or autumn or by seed sown in pots in early spring.

Growing—yarrow will grow in any soil in a sunny position.

Harvesting—cut the leaves and flowers for drying as the plant comes into flower.

Uses—a traditional medicinal herb with many applications.

THE HERB GARDENING CALENDAR

JAN	FEB	MAR	APR	MAY	JUNE	JULY	AUG	SEPT	OCT	NOV	DEC

Dig & compost
light soils

Mulch
established
gardens

Dig & compost
heavy soils

Plant
hardy herbs

Plant
half-hardy
herbs

Plant
hardy
herbs

Indoor
sowings

Outdoor
sowings

Outdoor
sowings

Weeding
(especially new gardens)

Water newly planted
& moisture-loving
herbs

Main herb
foliage harvest

Save
seed

Harvest
roots

Cut back old
shrubby herbs
severely

Summer clipping
pruning & staking

Cut down
old herbaceous
growth,
clear annuals

Give winter
protection where
necessary

Divide
herbaceous
herbs

Take soft-stem
cuttings

Take semi-ripe
cuttings

Divide
herbaceous
herbs

FURTHER READING

Herb cookery
Arabella Boxer and Phillipa Back, *The Herb Book* (Octopus, 1980, for Marks and Spencer plc). Contains many realistic yet appetizing recipes.

Martha Rose Shulman *Herb and Honey Cookery* (Thorsons 1984).

Herbal medicine
Juliette de Bairacli Levy, *The Illustrated Herbal Hand Book* (Faber Paperbacks, 1982). One of the most practical and reliable modern herbals.

Nalda Gosling, *Successful Herbal Remedies*, (Thorsons 1985).

Pot-pourri
Jacqueline Hériteau, *Pot-pourris and Other Fragrant Delights* (Penguin, 1982).

Herb gardens and gardening
Sarah Garland, *The Herb Garden* (Windward, 1984).
Elizabeth and Reginald Peplow, *A Complete Guide to the Herb Gardens of Great Britain* (Webb and Bower, 1984).

Garden construction
David L. Bebb, *Handyman Gardener* (Sundial Publications, 1979, for Marks and Spencer plc). Contains useful information on building raised beds, arches, ponds, etc. and laying paths.

USEFUL ADDRESSES

Organic gardening
Henry Doubleday Research Association, Ryton on Dunsmore, Coventry—an organization which carries out research into organic growing for amateur gardeners. Publishes a range of books and booklets, and supplies organic fertilizers, safe pesticides and some herb seeds. Runs the National Centre for Organic Gardening – display gardens demonstrating organic methods.

Herb suppliers
Suffolk Herbs, Sawyers Farm, Little Cornard, Sudbury, Suffolk. Supplies a wide range of herb seeds.

Herb nurseries supplying plants are now widespread, but the Herb Trades Association publishes a comprehensive list, available from Member Nurseries.

Correspondence Courses
The National Institute of Medical Herbalists, 148 Forest Road, Tunbridge Wells, Kent. Runs an excellent one year correspondence course for people wanting to use herbal remedies to treat minor ailments at home—no book can substitute for the understanding that it provides. The Institute also has a directory of qualified herbal practitioners.

INDEX

Achillea millefolium, see Yarrow
Agastache anethiodora, see Anise hyssop
Alchemilla mollis, see Lady's mantle
Alkaloids, 10
Allium cepa, see Tree onion
Allium sativum, see Garlic
Allium schoenaprasum, see Chives
Anethum graveolens, see Dill
Angelica, 14, 52, 68, 93
   harvesting stems, 54
Angelica archangelica, see Angelica
Anise hyssop, 94
Annual herbs, 12, 30, 38, 49
Anthemis nobilis, see Chamomile
Anthriscus cerefolium, see Chervil
Aphids, 50, 90
Applemint, 12, 109
Arbours, 26
Artemisia abrotanum, see Southernwood
Artemisia absinthium, see Wormwood
Artemisia dracunculus, see Tarragon

Bacillus thuringiensis, 52
Balsamita vulgaris, see Costmary
Basil, 63, 94
   drying, 56
   harvesting, 53
   in cooking, 63, 68
   oil, 70
Bay, 28, 44, 50, 85, 95
   scale insects on, 50
Bee herbs, 89
Biennial herbs, 12, 38, 49
Bergamot, 90, 95
   harvesting flowers, 54
   in pot-pourri, 82
   tea, 71
Biscuits, herb, 69
Bitters, 10
Blackberry, medicinal use, 76
Borage, 96
   harvesting flowers, 54
   in drinks, 71
   in the vegetable garden, 89
Borago officinalis, see Borage
Bouquet garni, 63
Bread, herb, 69

Brooklime, 28
Butter, herb, 70

Calendula officinalis, see Marigold
Caraway, 79, 96
Carrot fly, 50, 89
Cartwheel design, 21, 28
Carum carvi, see Caraway
Caterpillars, 50, 52
Catmint, 90
Chamomile, 97
   lawn, 23, 37
   medicinal and cosmetic use, 76, 78
Cheese, herbs with, 67
Chervil, 63, 98
Chequerboard design, 21
Chives, 29, 89-90, 98
   butter, 70
   freezing, 58
Chrysanthemum parthenium, see Feverfew
Climbers, 25
Cochlearia armoracia, see Horseradish
Comfrey, 98
   liquid feed, 91
   medicinal use, 77
   propagation, 45
   rust, 51
   use in potting compost, 86
Companion planting, 89
Compositae, 11, 12
Compress, 75
Compost, activaters, 91
   garden, 35
   seed sowing, 40
Constituents of herbs, 10
Coriander, 99
   harvesting, 53
Coriandrum sativum, see Coriander
Cosmetics, 77
Corsican mint, 23, 109
Costmary, 99
Cotton lavender, 26, 90, 100
Creeping herbs, 23
Curry plant, 27, 100
Cushions, herb, 83
Cuttings, 43-46

Decoction, 75
Derris, 52
Dill, 101
  freezing, 58
  harvesting, 53
  in the vegetable garden, 89
  medicinal use, 77
  vinegar, 70
Disease control, 50
Division, 45
Drainage, 17
Drying, 56-57

Eau-de-cologne mint, 81, 109
Edging herbs, 24
Eggs with herbs, 67
Elder, 101
  leaves as fungicide, 92
Elderflower champagne, 71
Elderflowers, harvesting, 54
  medicinal and cosmetic use, 73, 76
Eruca sativa, see Rocket

Fennel, 102
  bronze, 90, 102
  medicinal use, 77
Feverfew, 77, 102
Filipendula ulmaria, see Meadowsweet
Fines herbes, 63
Fixatives, 79, 81
Flowers, drying, 56
  harvesting, 54
Focal points, 27
Foeniculum vulgare, see Fennel
Foxglove, 9
Freezing herbs, 58

Garlic, 37, 61, 70, 102
  as a fungicide, 91
  medicinal use, 76, 77
Geraniums, scented, 81, 85, 103
Ginger mint, 109
Glycocides, 10
Good King Henry, 9

Hardening off, 46
Heartsease pansies, 29, 77, 103
Hedges, 17, 24-27
Hops, 27, 73, 77, 104
Horseradish, 76, 104
Hoverflies, 50, 90
Hyssop, 14, 26-27, 105

Infusion, 75
Iris florentina, see Orris

Labiates, 11, 12, 89
Ladybirds, 50

Lady's mantle, 90, 103
  medicinal use, 77
Laurus nobilis, see Bay
Lavendula, see Lavender
Lavender, 106
  as a bath herb, 78
  harvesting, 54
  hedge, 25-27
  in pot-pourri, 82
Layering, 44
Leaf miner, 50-51
Lemon balm, 71, 106
  medicinal use, 77
Lemon verbena, 14, 71, 85, 107
  in pot-pourri, 82
Levisticuna officinalis, see Lovage
Lippia citriodora, see Lemon verbena
Liquid feeding, 91
Lovage, 107
  in cooking, 66, 68-69
  in propagation, 45, 52

Manure, 35
Marigolds, 81, 108
  medicinal and cosmetic uses, 77, 78
Marjoram, 108
Matricaria, chamomilla, see Chamomile
Meadowsweet, 109
  medicinal use, 75, 77
Mellissa officinalis, see Lemon balm
Mentha, see Mint
Minerals, 76
Mint (see also Peppermint, Applemint, Corsican
  mint, Eau-de-cologne mint), 12, 35-36, 109
  in drinks, 71
  propagation, 44-46
  rust, 51
Monarda, see Bergamot
Mucilages, 10
Mulching, 50
Mullein, 76, 110
  freezing, 58
  moth, 50
Myrrhis odorata, see Sweet cicely

Naming herbs, 11
Nasturtium, 29, 110

Ocimum, see Basil
Offsets, 45
Oils, herb, 58
  aromatic, 10, 81-82
Origanum, see Marjoram
Orris, 111
  root, 81

Parsley, 11, 29, 63, 111
  drying, 56

harvesting, 53
medicinal use, 77
vitamins in, 76
Paths, 21
Paving slabs, 21
Pelargonium, see Geraniums
Peppermint, 12, 109
in pot-pourri, 82
Pest control, 50, 91
Petroselinum crispum, see Parsley
pH, 18
Pillows, herb, 83
Pineapple mint, 109
Pools, 28, 73-74
Potting compost, 80
Powdery mildew, 50
Poultice, 75
Pruning, 48-50

Raised beds, 26
Raspberry leaves, 77
Rocket, 53, 112
Roots, cuttings, 45
drying, 57
harvesting of, 56
Rosemary, 14, 27, 68, 113
biscuits, 69
cuttings, 43
pruning, 49-50
Roses, 25, 81, 82
Rosmarinus officinalis, see Rosemary
Rumex, see Sorrel
Rust, 51

Sage, 88, 113
drying, 56
medicinal and cosmetic use, 76-78
propagation, 43-45
pruning, 50
Salad burnet, 29, 68, 114
Salads, herb, 66-67
Salvia officinalis, see Sage
Sambucus nigra, see Elder
Sanguisorba minor, see Salad burnet
Santolina chamaecyparissus, see Cotton lavender
Saponins, 10
Satureia hortensis, see Savory (summer)
Satureia montana, see Savory (winter)
Savory (summer), 63, 114
(winter), 42, 63, 114
Scale insects, 50-52
Scones, herb, 69
Seats, herb, 26
Seaweed, liquid, 40, 47

Seedling crops, 53
Seeds, harvesting, 54-56
drying, 57
Skin conditioners, 78
Slugs, 50, 52
Soil acidity, 18
Sorrel, 50, 66-67, 115
Soups, herb, 66
Southernwood, 11, 27, 90, 115
Sowing seeds, 38-41
Spacing of herbs, 30
Spearmint, 109
Staking, 49
Stems, drying, 56
harvesting, 54
Storing dried herbs, 57
Sweet cicely, 54, 69, 116
Sweet dishes with herbs, 68
Symphytum, see Comfrey
Syrups, herb, 60

Tannins, 10
Tarragon, 116
drying, 56
in pots, 85
Thyme, 12, 117
creeping, 14, 23, 85, 117
jelly, 70
lemon, 12, 68, 71, 78, 117
medicinal use, 76, 77
propagation, 45
Thymus, see Thyme
Tincture, 75
Tree onion, 37, 117

Umbellifers, 11, 12, 50, 90

Vegetables, herbs with, 67
Vegetative propagation, 37
Verbascum thapsus, see Mullein
Vinegars, herb, 58-59
Viola tricolor, see Heartsease
Vitamins, 10, 76

Wall germander, 24, 27
Walls, 23, 24
Weeds, 33
Wormwood, 90, 118
for pest control, 92

Yarrow, 118
medicinal and cosmetic uses for, 73, 76, 78
Yellow flag, 28

Other titles in this series

PLANNING YOUR ORGANIC FLOWER GARDEN

Sue Stickland

ISBN 0 7225 1163 9
Paperback

PLANNING YOUR ORGANIC VEGETABLE GARDEN

Dick Kitto

ISBN 0 7225 1104 3
Paperback

MONTH-BY-MONTH ORGANIC GARDENING

Lawrence D. Hills

ISBN 0 7225 1863 3
Paperback